WHERE I LIVE NOW

*A Journey through Love
and Loss to Healing and Hope*

Sharon Butala

Phyllis Bruce Editions
Simon & Schuster Canada
New York   London   Toronto   Sydney   New Delhi

SIMON &
SCHUSTER
CANADA

Simon & Schuster Canada
A Division of Simon & Schuster, Inc.
166 King Street East, Suite 300
Toronto, Ontario M5A 1J3

This Simon & Schuster Canada edition December 2018

SIMON & SCHUSTER CANADA and colophon are
trademarks of Simon & Schuster, Inc.

For information about special discounts for bulk purchases,
please contact Simon & Schuster Special Sales at 1-800-268-3216
or customerservice@simonandschuster.ca.

Interior design by Lewelin Polanco

Manufactured in the United States of America

1 3 5 7 9 10 8 6 4 2

Library and Archives Canada Cataloguing in Publication

Butala, Sharon, 1940-, author
Where I live now : a journey through love and loss to healing and hope /
Sharon Butala.
Reprint. Originally published in hardcover in 2017.
Includes bibliographical references.
ISBN 978-1-982117-90-0 (softcover)
1. Butala, Sharon, 1940-. 2. Butala, Sharon, 1940- —Homes and haunts—
Saskatchewan. 3. Authors, Canadian (English)—20th century—Biography.
4. Moving, Household—Psychological aspects. 5. Bereavement. 6. Prairie
Provinces—Biography. 7. Autobiographies. I. Title.
PS8553.U6967Z46 2018   C813'.54   C2018-905409-3

ISBN 978-1-4767-9048-0
ISBN 978-1-9821-1790-0 (pbk)
ISBN 978-1-4767-9050-3 (ebook)

In
Memory
of
Kathleen Margaret (Le Blanc) Hollands
1949–2014

Contents

Sharon in her father's arms circa 1942.

Preface

Where I Live Now

In 1994 I published a memoir called *The Perfection of the Morning: An Apprenticeship in Nature*. It was my eighth book, my first non-fiction, and to this day the best-received and most successful of my books. I take little credit for this: Phyllis Bruce, my editor, took a small manuscript about building a relationship with nature and encouraged me to turn it into a narrative about a life lived on the land, and then we sent the memoir out into Canada having no idea — or at least, I certainly didn't — of what to expect in terms of response. I went off to Italy with my older sister something like the day after it was released, and after a week in Rome and a few days in Florence, while visiting in my sister's sister-in-law's house in the Friuli countryside about an hour from Venice, I phoned home. My husband told me that my literary agent and Phyllis had called to congratulate me because the book was on the Canadian bestseller list, I think then at number four. By early July it had gone to number one; it would stay on the list for a year. I'm telling you this not so much to brag — I still have a faintly stunned look on my face when I think of it — but to provide you with background to this book before you.

When I say I take little credit for that book's success, I mean that sometimes such a response is not so much that the book in question is brilliantly written or wonderfully astute and incisive. It is simply the right book at the right moment. Inadvertently (or perhaps not so inadvertently), a writer has something to say that is exactly what the reading public is parched for, and when such a book happens to appear, everybody clamours to read it. Much as I want to believe that *The Perfection of the Morning* was a work of genius, I know that it was what it was (not for me to judge) and that it was one of these books I've been describing.

At that point I had been living on my husband's cattle ranch and on the hay farm (forty miles — nothing in that vast country — northeast of the ranch) for around twenty years, having come from the small city of Saskatoon, where I'd been working on a graduate degree and teaching at the University of Saskatchewan.

I do not come from a distinguished academic family. I believe I was the first to teach at a university, but within months and then years I was leapfrogged over by a cousin who earned the first PhD, and soon by the unstoppable and ebullient younger generation, and now by their children, so that graduate degrees in the family today are fairly prosaic. All of this is to say that it was unexpected that I would one day simply walk away from that esteemed life and a respected university position and go to live on a remote cattle ranch located in the extreme southwest corner of Saskatchewan only a few miles from the Montana and Alberta borders. The ranch is situated on the Old Man On His Back Plateau — the naming is Blackfoot or Siksika and refers to their cultural hero, Napi, who is the "Old Man" of both the plateau and the river in Alberta. In some way I don't fully understand, the plateau is Napi's body, or it is the mark or formation left from the time that he lay there, weary and bleeding from battle, before he rose and went west to disappear into the mountains. *One day he will return*, I am told, is how the rest of the story goes, although to the First Nations people to whom this story belongs, it is not merely a story, but traditional belief. I would never get over the thrill of knowing that now I lived in such a potent place.

No one could understand our marriage, no one in Peter's world and no one in mine: Peter's friends and family said it wouldn't last a year, and mine, being slightly more optimistic, gave it two years. I was a "city girl," and city girls were famously feckless when it came to milking cows and chasing them around on horseback, to helping deliver calves, to understanding the seasonal round of work, or to telling one grass from another or poisonous forbs from nutritious ones, work utterly vital to the cattle enterprise. Nor were they able to stay on horseback for ten hours at a stretch, or to know in a treeless country how to lie low in the tall grass out of the wind to keep warm.

And the history! Every moment of every day we lived in the midst of the settlers' past where no piece of land, no falling-down empty house or shack was without a story, nearly always about heart-breaking hardship overcome, or about the saddest failure, the ignominious, broken departure from the land. Occasionally, many years later, I would meet a man whose story I'd been told — one of those who had had to leave his land. I would be rendered speechless by the meeting of myth and reality. All of this was a lesson in stories.

What Peter and I shared, as this book will tell, was a deep love of and respect for the beauty of nature and its ineffable mystery, the wonder of the deer, moose, pronghorns, occasional elk, the coyotes and foxes, all the way down to little creatures that ran the banks of the Frenchman River at the hay farm, the schools of fish that swam in it, and the snakes of sometimes astonishing size. Great birds came and went: pelicans, wild swans, ducks and geese and eagles, both golden and bald, and snowy owls, and songbirds — red-winged blackbirds and bluebirds and meadowlarks. We lived for the smell of the prairie in the spring, for the way the leaves of a certain grass curled, or made eyebrows, or another turned mauve for a few days on its way to maturity. We loved the buffalo horn casings we dug up out of the prairie, the stone flakes and artifacts from centuries ago. We loved the moon and the wheeling constellations and the way the coulees ran musically with melting snow in the spring. I think we loved even the howling blizzards and the sucking mud and the rocks scattered everywhere by melting glaciers.

But as the years passed, slowly, one after the other, not with neat calendar breaks but seamlessly in an eternal round of being and doing, a life lived under the stars and the endless sky, in the constant wind, through killing blizzards and summer storms that cracked and bellowed, and lit the sky from horizon to horizon, and periods of such intense cold or equally intense summer heat, I began to feel my mind, my heart, my soul — all of them — being slowly opened so that the boundary between me and these things melted, dissolved. Through awe-inspiring dreams, eventually through small visions, the Great Mystery of our being became clearer to me. Not the answer, but the question — the eternal question.

I had to re-educate myself. I learned not just about grasses, forbs, shrubs, or rocks, lichen and moss, or land formations or birthing calves or diseases of cattle, or the wild animals of the plains, but about the further history, the very long one of the Indigenous people (in Canada we say, at their request, the "First Nations") whose land we were living on. This vast, empty, grassed land filled up with stories: the easy ones — of settlers, government policies, agricultural changes — and the very hard, long First Nations' ones.

All of this is what that small book, *The Perfection of the Morning*, was about. How living on the land as thoroughly as we did, as completely as we did, changed us, or changed *me*. The book was about *me* learning to live in nature. In this I was taught the practicalities by Peter, my husband, by my books, by what I learned walking over the unplowed prairie every day for many years and, most of all, by the things I saw out on the land that I knew weren't "really there," though they once had been, and by my dreaming. There, in an excess of wonder and bafflement, rage and desire, I became a writer.

Thirty-three years I lived on those plains in the end, thirty-one as Peter's wife. A relatively young divorcée and single parent of thirty-six turned into a sixty-eight-year-old grandmother. It was a terrible life; it was an enchanted life; it was a blessed life.

And, of course, one day it ended.

There would be for me, I would find, no "normal" life after that; I would live the rest of my years in the shadow of that world. This is what this book is about, both the leaving and the sorrow and unending grief, and the inscrutable undertakings of fate and the future.

FORSAKEN

Sharon and Peter at the hay farm circa 1990.

1

The Cemetery

Often as I lie down in my bed, pull up the covers, and put out the light, settling in to spend another night alone here in Calgary, Alberta, I yearn to have my husband, Peter, with me again. I yearn not to be alone. But that is an old story, and among people in the last third of their lives, it is anything but unique. But, still, I lie at night and think of the past. I dream of it too — our life on the Great Plains to the east — and when I do, I wake filled with sadness. Once in a while a tiny part of me will for an instant take me over, allowing me to imagine there is a way to regain the past, but then reality returns, and my inner voice says, *You know as well as you know anything on earth that he is gone forever.* And yet, I am not sure I truly believe it.

I try to visit my husband's grave at least once a year, sometimes twice a year, although never in winter. When Peter died, I thought that as I wouldn't be able to keep on living in Saskatchewan, I would be faithful about my twice-yearly visits to his grave for at least the next ten years; after that, my imagination gave up. Some part of me probably thought that in ten years I would most likely be dead myself. When I imagined my own demise I could only think in terms of statistics. I stopped short when it came to the nursing home, the fatal illness, the final suffering, my last, shuddering breath.

When I make my private pilgrimage, I don't let anyone know I am coming. It takes about seven hours from Calgary, including at least a half hour to get out of the city and another for fuel and bathroom stops, and I need to stay overnight before I make the long drive back. When I start from Calgary I am filled with determination to complete what I see as my duty to Peter (as if he were still alive and monitoring my faithfulness), and I do my best not to think but only to concentrate on the traffic and the road, but all the while some strong emotion is building inside me. I drive the first three predictable hours (farms mostly, or fields of grass, usually pretty heavily grazed, a few head of cattle in the far distance, oil batteries, railway lines) on the high-speed, busy Trans-Canada Highway to Medicine Hat, where I make my usual stop to stretch my legs, buy gas, and buy food to take on the road with me.

Then I continue east, and about an hour after having crossed into Saskatchewan, I turn south toward Maple Creek, go west through the town and onto the secondary highway heading south. Here I am able to go more slowly, as the road narrows and the speed limit drops. Finally, almost no one else is on the road; I can take my time as I drive through the familiar, once much-loved countryside. Now I can no longer fully control the emotions I've been keeping at bay. They begin to grow and rise and will soon threaten to overwhelm me.

Something like eighteen miles south of the town, having climbed most of the way, I reach the gate into Cypress Hills Interprovincial Park, but for some miles before, I can see the park along the horizon on the western side of the road. It is easily recognizable because in a landscape where most of the year the fields and hills are the pale yellow and buff of cured grass, its high, pine-covered hills, dark blue-black with hints of deep green, stand out. In a country otherwise sparsely treed except for the deciduous ones planted in neat rows by settlers in their farmyards, the attraction of these immensely tall, though thinly limbed, lodgepole pines in a park that is the highest point between the Rockies and Labrador is understandable.

The park rises about 2,000 feet (600 metres) above the high plains, and stretches from Saskatchewan into Alberta. It is treed as a result of the glaciers having spared the highest part; here montane species of plants still grow that occur nowhere else in the province. From sea level, the highest point is in the Alberta portion of the Cypress Hills and is roughly 4,800 feet; in Saskatchewan, it is about 4,500 feet. It's only when you get to the Lookout on the far west side of the park that you see how high you are.

On these trips I rarely pass by the gate without driving in, and sometimes, if I've thought to buy a lunch in Medicine Hat, I may find a picnic table somewhere and eat my sandwiches under the trees, my feet resting on grass instead of a sticky restaurant floor, and my head filled with pine scent and the cool, fresh, welcoming air hinting of the wild. I was born in the forested, lake-dotted country to the north where such vistas are commonplace, and I find these pines a welcome break from the miles of treeless, anonymous country I've just come through. I often contemplate how strange it is that I fell so in love with a terrain and ground cover so completely different from the one I was born into and where I first knew life.

I often think that my sisters and I came out of legend. Our childhood in the northern bush is so linked with fear — of the extreme cold and deep snow, of the dark trackless forest all around us, of the

Indigenous peoples who had their own ways, who did not speak our language, indeed, who rarely spoke — that I chose as a writer to turn my beginnings into a dark myth. I saw too the paucity of the conditions under which we lived, our mother's youthful gaiety slowly overtaken by disappointment and anger, our father's bewildered, helpless retreat.

When I was just school age we left that part of the country forever, moving gradually to larger towns and then to a small city. I tried to forget the wilderness, believing then that people could forget where they began, as if it were merely a mistake. But I know now that our childhoods mark us forever, and that to view such happenings in a life as mere mistakes, as simple bad choices, is in itself a mistake. Where we start life marks us irreparably. More than twenty years later, a marriage, a child, a divorce, and moves across the country and back again behind me, at thirty-six I married Peter and went to his ranch home in Saskatchewan on the high Great Plains of North America to live out the rest of my life. And yet, that archetypal forest I was born into hovered there relentlessly, dark and heavy, in the back of my brain. Cypress Hills Park, then, has seemed only to hint at that forbidding landscape from my childhood.

I sometimes take the time to drive up to the highest point at the Lookout where, in three directions and a few hundred feet below, I see fields and more fields, sprinkled with grazing cattle, mere dark points on the pale aqua, buff, and cream grass, the colours exquisitely softened by distance and haze until at some far-off edgeless place they simply meld into the pale bottom of the sky, become indistinguishable from it. The wind catches you up there, sweeping across miles of prairie and smelling of burning sun and grasses, sage and pine, and flowering bushes. The far-distant world below that I'm scrutinizing is, from this vantage point, fairy-tale beautiful, and it is a wonder to me that the society it supports should sometimes be so unforgiving, so brutal to its dwellers.

Although from where I was in the park I couldn't see it, a few miles to the east in the wooded hills on the other side of the highway, still part of the Cypress Hills, is the Nekaneet First Nation. It would be many years after I moved to the southwest before I would even set foot on the reserve itself and then it was, briefly, to volunteer at the new Okimaw Ohci Healing Lodge, a prison for federally sentenced Aboriginal women where I and a number of other farm and ranch women were to provide some "normalcy" in the lives of those women, some of whom had been incarcerated many years, and others who would soon be released to go back into society. I think the idea was that we would remind them of how to be with women out in general society. I also taught a creative writing workshop, where I wound up mostly dealing with the single white woman prisoner there, about whom, after she was released and died of ALS, a film was made. The other prisoner I saw the most of was a Cree woman, one who had collaborated as a co-author in a book about her life. I never thought of them as prisoners, though, but rather as people I knew and liked (both had committed murders, although the white woman would eventually receive a special dispensation and be released early as a victim of severe marital abuse). I would have kept them both as friends had the justice system allowed such a thing, and if one hadn't died so soon after her release.

It is told that when a site for the lodge was being searched for, a committee of elders was struck, and one of them had a dream telling all of them that this was where it should be built — in the place they called the Thunder Breeding Hills. It is gratifying to think that is how the site was chosen. When I first saw the reserve, appearing as a horizontal white line high in the treed hills miles south of Maple Creek that, as you drew closer, would separate into buildings, it was poor and barely known by most of the local people unless they had land near it. The relationship of the townspeople to the people of the reserve seemed to me then fraught with tension and, to some extent, mutual dislike and mistrust. Then

the people of the reserve had their land claims settled, and exciting
things started to happen, the building of the healing lodge being
only one of them.

Once, these people travelled all over this vast land, without any
barriers or park signs or jails, following their ancestral trails. As
the settlement era began in the West in the late 1800s, treaties between the European newcomers (many from Eastern Canada and
the United States) were signed that drove Indigenous peoples of the
plains onto small reserves. Treaty 4, signed in 1874, moved them
south of the South Saskatchewan River, to the north, or east of the
city of Regina. Only a small band of people led by a man named
Nekaneet (or "foremost man") remained behind in the Cypress
Hills, living on game and otherwise making do for many years until
in 1913 the government granted them a small reserve in the hills,
later expanded. The rewards of signing these treaty documents were
laughable, and in the late twentieth century such high-handedness
and injustice to the First Nations people were at last addressed in
the form of land claims designed to return much of the ancestral
lands to the descendants of the original inhabitants. The Nekaneet
people didn't receive the right to be included in the land claims
process until 1998.

South I go now, until I come to the gravel road that threads its
way east and south to the village of Eastend. With some regret I
pass it by. On these drives to visit Peter's grave, I rarely take that
cross-country route, even though it cuts about twenty miles from
the already long trip. On my move to the city, I sold our large SUV,
opting instead for a more manageable small car, the first vehicle in
my entire life that I had bought myself. Inexperienced as I was, I
didn't notice that its clearance was too low to allow me to risk gravel

roads, so on these trips to Peter's grave I usually go around the long way on the paved roads. The drive descends most of the way, the hills rising up on my left or to the east. If you know where to look, you can see cairns and other more enigmatic stone structures made by the First Nations people in past centuries, some of them visible as small protuberances along the skyline.

About forty miles south of Maple Creek, never having left a paved road, I turn east again on the highway into Eastend. In those first years after I moved away, my heart would start to ache as I left Medicine Hat, as I have told you. I would feel as if my chest and throat were filling with dark water, making an aching lump of them. Once I turned to go south at Maple Creek the pain would worsen, the water struggling to erupt from my eyes. When I made that last turn east to start the thirty-five or so miles into Eastend, I would be in full-blown pain, anger tinged equally with bitterness, bitterness that I otherwise kept at bay, but that never failed to overtake me as I neared my husband's grave. Now the tears are gone, although a residue of pain remains.

Deep in the south country, heading east, on my right and another twenty miles to the south, lies what has been since 1910 or so the vast Butala cattle ranch. I can't actually see it from that distance, because those many hectares of low rolling hills characteristic of the area intervene. But I know it is there, and think of the many times I had looked out the cracked kitchen window (a window Peter told me his mother had, years earlier, importuned her husband to put in because she felt cut off not being able to see in that direction) and gazed north, imagining trucks driving east or west on this very road. Sometimes, Peter said, on a really clear night, there would be places between the hills where from the ranch, there being not a single dwelling between the kitchen and the road twenty miles to the north, you could see the headlights of a vehicle. I'd seen one myself, that moving light travelling like a tiny spaceship through the darkness below the millions of stars.

This is when the longing I'm experiencing — or maybe it isn't longing, as I don't quite allow myself to long — this is when the pain and sorrow I'm experiencing are at their worst.

My emotions are so mixed I hardly know what to make of them myself; I only know they make me feel badly enough to want never to make this trip again. On the one hand, I suffered from extreme loneliness for many years in this country. On the other hand, the beauty of the land, the peace and simplicity of the life, even the roughness, and the doing without (high culture, congenial companions, a bathroom!) taught me a lot. Above all, there was the joy of being someone's partner in life, someone for whom and from whom there was respect and love. This is the turmoil I experience every single time I make this trip. I suppose Joan Didion would call it grief, but it is, in fact, so much more than that. And who knows what Didion experienced that she chose not to put into *The Year of Magical Thinking*, her celebrated memoir about the year that began with her husband's sudden death. Didion is, as Peter was, famously cryptic, famously silent.

A few miles past the place where I turned east, I come to the cattle gate that leads into the provincial pasture, a one-hundred-section area (a section is a mile by a mile), I think the biggest in the province, that borders on the west and the north of what had been the Butala ranch. I can't see the gate from the road I am on, only the trail off the road; on the other side of a low rise you will bump over the cattle gate and then be in the pasture, and if you know which trail to take and keep going, winding in and out around the grassy hills, leaving the trail in places where rain or melted snow has made it impassable for twenty or fifty feet or, in wet springs, maybe even longer distances, going through other gates, past waterholes or large troughs where the water was pumped up by windmills or, in later years, by solar panels, with cattle clustered around them, eventually you will reach the gate that opens onto the Butala land less than a mile from the house. But you'd be a fool to try it if you didn't know the country, and if it had been raining and you didn't have four-wheel drive and a lot of experience driving under such conditions. By the time my years in the southwest were over, I had made that drive by myself a couple of times. I think I should be proud of that even if I did it only in the driest times, but I am, I find, more saddened to remember, because I remember too that I went alone.

We used to ride horses out there occasionally; we had as a destination a particular hill, the highest in that huge area, the size of a tiny European country, and we would climb to the top on horseback, steering the horses on a zigzag pattern up the hill to make it easier on them. You had to hang on to your saddle blanket, too, because while you climbed it might work its way out from under the saddle, and in that vast space you would never find it again. Riding to the very top was an adventure. We never had much to say when we got there; usually nobody spoke, but each wandered off around the relatively flat space and gazed off into the distance as if, suddenly, an imperial city might be seen along the misty horizon, or an army on the move with troops and tanks and trucks. But there was nothing of the sort: just more hills, more grass, in the far distance the thin green snake of a windbreak of caraganas around somebody's farmhouse, and sometimes the faint blue of the Bears Paw Mountains in Montana or a hint that might have been the Sweet Grass Hills to the southwest. We would look down at the tiny prairie plants, turn over a small stone, or gaze in thoughtful silence at the ancient pile of rocks some forgotten Indigenous people had long ago placed there.

I still have an arrowhead given to me by somebody who rode with us once. He had found it on the edge of a slough at the bottom of the hill. So much of that life has gone from me that I wonder why I even keep that arrowhead: I never look at it anymore, and it is so tiny compared to the weight of memory; yet I keep it. I remember that the person who found it said to me, touching his solar plexus, "You have to *give up* something to find them." But I seem to have given up the wrong things: I used to find scrapers and flakes (tools for cleaning hides and the remnants of the tool-making) all over the place, but not arrowheads, or "points," as the archaeologists call them.

Driving slowly by on the highway, knowing what lies on the other side of that low rise, the wind, the moving grass, the stars, the ghosts of the plains people of the past, the wild, I know that I will never again make that meandering drive among the hills and the cattle and the echoes of the past. So I keep on going east resolutely, and eventually the road curves north and the extreme east end of the Cypress Hills begins to rise before me, at first on my left and then straight ahead, extending just a little to my right, where, with surprising abruptness, the hills terminate. Just before the curve in the road leading down into the valley and the town, I reach the trail that leads into the cemetery where Peter's remains lie.

By the time I reach the approach to the cemetery, it is usually late afternoon or even early evening. I don't stop but keep on driving through Eastend and on into the next town, where I spend the night in a hotel. I don't sleep well; I suffer on these trips from a high level of tension, some of it inexplicable — what is it I am afraid of? — but most of it caused by the memories I cannot push back out of sight, memories that I can't shake off no matter how tired I am. Because of this I rise very early, the long blue shadows of night still vying with the liquid gold slowly spreading across the fields, gather my few things, check out, get in my car, and head back west on the road I came in on the evening before, continue on through the sleeping village of Eastend, climb up the road out of town, and turn in at the cemetery set on a sloping plateau high above the village on the south side of the Frenchman River valley.

When Peter died and I finally got to that stage of grief where I could think about my own future, I figured I had about ten years left to live. With that ten-year limit in my mind, and the fact that the village has a cemetery society to cut the grass, gather dried-out bouquets and throw out the plastic ones the weather has destroyed, as well as to inform the living if their loved one's headstone needs to be re-set or if the grave is sinking, and given that Peter never really leaves my mind and heart, that he is embedded forever in my dreams and in my soul, I have to wonder why it matters to me to make these visits, to go out of my way not to see anyone in the community. Why am I there?

I park my car out of sight behind a low hill, and when I've shut off the motor and climbed out, I stand still for a moment, the breeze playing around me, and look around at the clumps of pasture sage, the grass-covered hillside rising behind me, across the valley to the glass-fronted T.rex Discovery Centre high on the other side, and up the valley to the west and then to the east. It is a peaceful setting. I can smell the sage, enjoy the sun whose realm I sense so high above the town. I have brought flowers, tiger lilies if I can get them, or other hothouse flowers associated with the prairie — daisies or snapdragons, small sunflowers. I bring a jug of water, a brush, a cloth, in order to wipe the bird droppings off the headstone, to clean the dirt off the base, and to shine the part the tombstone maker had polished to a perfect gleaming surface, leaving the sides as rough stone.

I go slowly up the hillside along the long row of lilac bushes and the fence that make the eastern boundary, passing graves of people whose names I recognize. Sometimes I remember a face, note one or two freshly dug graves, some with only temporary markers, and then I see Peter's stone up ahead, on my right. I never know what to feel when I see it, and sometimes I hurry those last few feet as if he is sitting there lazily on his headstone, swinging one leg from the knee, braced on the other one, that easy-going, welcoming expression on his face, waiting for me to reach him.

But he is never there: I stand beside the headstone and the grave looking down at the pale grey-beige earth, the grass beginning to grow around and on it, at the red-speckled brown headstone I chose with such care, the stone that came from India, and I wait to feel something meaningful beyond what I guess is grief and the other emotions widows feel: regret; anger over old wounds, misunderstandings, and failures; warmth over remembered intimacy and tenderness; sadness for the sharing that is gone forever. I've never been good at obvious grief — the prostration, the sobbing, the retreat into deep, stone-like depression. I think too much, I go over and over events from the past as if by re-thinking and re-thinking them I can finally tease out from between the strands of memory, intertwined as they are, the real meaning, the answers to the questions that I don't even know to ask. He was my husband for thirty-one years; I have a lot of things to mull over in my mind. Didion is never sentimental, and I like to think that I am not sentimental, and I know that visiting a grave annually or semi-annually is a sentimental thing to do, and yet I continue to do it.

From the beginning of my widowhood I had a strong need to do everything the right way. We did not cremate Peter — cremation seemed wrong to me; I felt he had done enough for his country that he deserved a fine, old-fashioned funeral and a grave in the Eastend cemetery with a good-quality tombstone with his name cut into it so that a century might pass before his name was lost. His father and his mother are both in that graveyard, and a lot of other people who were his neighbours and friends long before I married him. As well, as in most country cemeteries, there is a row of small stones of the children of one family who died all at the same time — in a fire, most likely, or maybe of diphtheria or scarlet fever — children no one now living ever saw, even their story lost. So I had his name and dates and RANCHER — OLD MAN ON HIS BACK engraved on the stone's front and on the back FAR-SEEING (and never mind the puzzle over how to spell *far-seeing*). I took a cue from his mother, who, when her husband, Peter's father, died, had a beautiful tombstone erected at his grave and had carved on it the words RANCHER and SMOLNIK, CZECHOSLOVAKIA, the village from where he had come in 1913 (now in the Slovak Republic). Respecting Peter's heritage is important to me too.

Once I've finished polishing the stone and sweeping the dirt away from the footings, and have put the flowers into the plastic vase and pushed it into the earth in front of his headstone, I am at a loss as to what to do. In order to be properly respectful, I go to his parents' graves and then to the graves of the few people buried there whom I actually knew myself, the number of these having increased every time I return. Then I head back to the car; stow my whisk broom, water jug, and cloth; get back in; and, with great reluctance and even greater puzzlement, the town still not stirring except for the one or two farm trucks on the road heading early out to the land, I start the long drive back to the city. I drive away fast, as if I am being pursued.

I do not mourn much on the way home, either for the lost land and the grass and flowering plants, the hills and the sky, or for Peter. My grief has been satiated for a while. Again I ask myself: Why do I do this? It takes two full days out of my busy life, and enormous emotional energy, and makes no difference at all that I can see. If nobody in the community even knows I was there, my trips can't be to satisfy their requirements as to what makes a faithful wife. Most of the local people, these days, are cremated, in any case, and I have no idea what is done with their ashes but suspect that as a result there is nobody to visit *in* the graveyard, the remains being kept elsewhere or having been scattered to the winds. Still, I am doing my duty, whether Peter, or his dead parents, or his siblings, or anyone else cares or not. Maybe the ritual comforts me. I am still trying to answer the question I asked when I first came to the southwest: What am I doing here in this place so different from the one into which I was born and so far from the world of achievement I lived in before I gave it up to marry Peter? What was I doing here for thirty-three years? Maybe I hope that if I keep coming here year after year, somehow, someday, Peter will answer me.

I don't waste any time until I reach Medicine Hat nearly three hours later; then I stop, eat, buy gas, and begin the last three hours of my drive into Calgary at as leisurely a pace as the Trans-Canada Highway allows. After two hours of heading northwest, I turn west and take a smaller paved highway on which you can't go faster than one hundred kilometres per hour and sometimes not faster than fifty, that runs through the Siksika (or Blackfoot) reserve, then through the countryside below a line of villages that mostly can't be seen from the road, and past cropland and farmhouses and round steel granaries, fields of grass and stands of tall, healthy leafy green poplars and elm trees, until finally I reach the highway that runs east–west along the southern edge of the city. On your right as you approach the city's boundaries you can see the downtown high-rises, faded blue and purple with glimmers of gold rising above the flatland, and often when the weather is just right, straight ahead the dramatic snow-capped, peaked line of the Rocky Mountains. Even the air feels different, crisper, harder. When I first took that route, the road was just a normal if busy city thoroughfare, but now it is six lanes in places, fast, with many overpasses, exits, and feeder roads, and is called, ironically, Stoney Trail, after the Nakoda, or Stoney, people, who have a nearby reserve. For the slow and nervous driver there is no longer any mercy, but I grit my teeth and drive it.

This is home now. But although I had to move to the city when Peter died, I did so with reluctance, seeing my fate as sealed by his very death and just as much by my being a woman in a man's world. Yet that part of the Great Plains was my home for so many years, and there is still a part of me that has not left and never will. With this memoir, I hereby claim forever my portion of that country whose many layers of history still resonate in my imagination — a place where wind and sun ruled and where it was, in those days, sometimes so dry that even the bitterly cold winter months could be nearly snowless. It was here on the open, treeless plains of southwest Saskatchewan, I lived what turned out to be not the rest of my life, but only the middle, the fulcrum, around which everything else circles.

2

The Ghost in the Trees

I always thought that I would die first (this despite the fact that I was six years younger than Peter). Perhaps it was his ability to endure, his sense of being at home in the world. I did know, though, without any doubt, I would not be able to stay on the land. I couldn't manage a ranch or work a hay farm myself, and I didn't even want to try, and in those days it was unheard of to let agricultural land lie fallow, as I would choose to do. I knew also that loneliness would drag me down, and although more than once it was suggested to me that the hay farm would make a great writers' colony, when I thought of the work involved and possibly the disapproval of the neighbours, I just couldn't face such an idea. No, I would have to leave. I didn't worry about where I would go, though, as I had close family in several places in the West. And anyway, it was all so far in the future that it was foolish to waste time contemplating such a decision.

But behind Peter's hardiness was a weakness. Since he was a young man, Peter had had stomach pains that were not accounted for. As our years together passed slowly, what turned out to be his acid reflux condition grew worse and worse. It was discovered that he had a hiatus hernia, and swallowing began to be more difficult. Eventually, during most of one year, he began to throw up his meals, and he took various medications and began to undergo various medical tests.

On the fourth of June, 2006 (we had returned from a long trip to Australia and New Zealand in late January), our family doctor told him that he had esophageal cancer. I had understood this a few days earlier, but when I tried to explain that this was what the nurse at the Medicine Hat imaging clinic was telling him in her round-about gentle way, he wouldn't believe me, or perhaps he simply couldn't bear to hear me, and I felt it better not to insist. But the following Monday, when we saw his family physician, he could no longer deny it. Thus began, as all readers will know, a terrible time for him that would end in his death, and also a very difficult time for me as I tried to support him, nurse him, drive him, comfort him, and help him eat, always trying to find something that he could actually swallow as his condition worsened. Then the time came when he could swallow nothing, not even water, and the trips to the hospitals began.

It was summer by then, and many of the staff members of our neighbouring hospitals, including doctors and specialists, were away on holiday, making it necessary for our local physician to spend time on the telephone trying to find a hospital a reasonable distance away with a staff gastroenterologist or cardiologist to see him. After each foray to Regina or Saskatoon, we would return to our home and Peter would have to be, in an emergency situation, driven by me to the hospital in a nearby town to be given intravenous fluids or whatever the physician decreed. Sometimes he did not know where he was and would whisper this to me, and I would tell him. I was not always sure that what I said helped, although mainly it did. If it seems now to me that in some ways this went on forever, an eternity of our driving down empty highways in the high summer heat to large, unwelcoming, and very noisy city hospitals, it seems in other ways to have been only days from the diagnosis to his death two months later. I had cancelled my few summer's engagements at festivals and conferences, and I gave myself over to his needs. Not that I was much use to him, except as someone who was always there at his side through the rest of this journey.

Almost immediately following his diagnosis surgery was planned for him, an operation described by one surgeon to me as "one of the biggest we do," a really frightening prospect. Peter was booked for this procedure in three weeks, but when the time came, he failed his pre-surgery evaluation. The cancer had moved too fast and it was too late.

Three or four times in the next couple of days, someone, each a different expert in his field, came and stood at the foot of his bed and carefully confirmed the verdict: Too late for surgery, no other procedure suitable. In the end, as far as I can tell, little could be done to prevent his dying or even to slow it. There were attempts to make him comfortable and, at least twice, a ghastly procedure to open his throat so that he could swallow a little, for a while. Then, without further ceremony, he was sent home to die. "Home," in this case, was, at Peter's own choice, the twenty-some-bed hospital in the town twenty-five miles from our home.

In those last days, once Peter was settled in the palliative care room, I would spend the night at home, rising early to arrive back there by about seven and staying at the hospital until visiting hours came in the evening. By this time, I had been through the death of loved ones three other times, and the process was familiar to me. I actually believed, because this had been my experience with my father, then my mother and then with a sister, that this stage would go on for several months and that I needed to ration my strength for that long road. Even though we had been told Peter would not survive his cancer (looking back, I know that Peter had with great reluctance accepted that this was true), nobody had ever said directly to me, "Your husband is dying. He won't survive more than a few weeks." So I went on pretending to myself for days that it wasn't true. For three nights I drove home through the gold of the early August evenings, arriving in time to feed the barn and house cats, talk to the horses, walk outside in the evening stillness for a few minutes, then spend a couple of hours phoning family and friends to report on Peter's condition.

The house, those nights, felt magical. It felt as if it were someone else's house, the shadows in the corners rounded and soft, as the day melted into night, the pools of light golden, the edges alive where light softened and mingled with dark, and outside, glowing silver-blue and resonant. My last phone call made, I would fall into bed and sleep soundly without a single dream and wake too early at five or so, still exhausted, frantic to get back to the hospital.

The first morning when I was rushing through the kitchen into the sun porch to speed to the hospital, I saw that two of the window screens had been pushed into the porch and that there was now nothing to keep out birds and animals. Before I'd gone to bed I had opened all the windows to capture the night's coolness, and the interior screens were held in place only by those little plastic arms in strategic spots around their perimeters, each at the most a half inch long. Now the screens lay awkwardly half on and half off the furniture. This was peculiar: there'd been no wind overnight, only that steady bath of heat, and even in my frozen state, absent even from my own terror, I was sure I couldn't possibly have done it myself. Fortunately, though, defeating my purpose in keeping the windows open, I had closed and locked the door between the porch and the kitchen before I went to bed.

WHERE I LIVE NOW

The second morning the screens were down again, only this time they didn't lie where they had fallen, but were scattered about the room. What was going on? But in a rush, my mind in a turmoil, I simply put the screens back up and hurried on to the hospital. The third morning one screen was again down. Now this had become a mystery, and as I rushed over the country roads, tires crackling and spitting gravel, I thought and thought about it, and finally it came to me: Raccoons! Of course, it had been raccoons all along: the clever little beasts with their unnervingly strong fingers could easily have done it. Thankfully, I hadn't told anyone, and I felt foolish over what I began to see was my full-blown paranoia.

I was no longer myself, was not fully present to anything. I felt as if I were holding my breath, had been doing so for days and then, as time passed, for weeks. I ran back and forth each night, reporting faithfully on Peter's condition, holding back my emotions because a part of me knew that if allowed out they would knock me to my knees, would render me useless. I was in time and yet outside it. I can't remember now if Peter asked me to stay all night at the hospital, his last two nights on earth. When the moment of his death finally came in the late afternoon, not at night, I was there, holding him for those long moments — they seemed forever — until he departed.

I might still have been holding his head as I had done for the last half hour or so of his struggle — such a current of heat there was flowing between the back of his neck and my fingers during that time! — I can't remember. I know I kissed him and I stood looking into the face of the man to whom I had been married for so many years, waiting for the facial contortion of the struggle and suffering of his death to subside; I would not leave him until I had seen one last time the face that I had known as his. I thought only that if I waited another moment his real face would return, and then I would be able to leave him.

But instead, as I watched, his face began to change, and to

change again, and to change again, and again, and again. Aghast, unable to look away, I saw his jaw thin and narrow, his teeth get smaller and more even, his cheekbones get higher and more prominent, his skin begin to stretch tightly over the newly shaped bones of his face, until what I saw in the end was the face of . . . I couldn't say exactly, but it seemed to me that it was the face of a Mongolian warlord, or no — it was an Asian face, maybe the face of a high priest — perhaps a Buddhist monk was a better description. Either way, what I saw now was the composed death mask of a stranger, not of the work-ruined rural peasant attaining peace in death, or the contemporary temple scholar, pale and other-worldly, but of someone of power and wisdom.

Deeply shaken and yet also in pain because it seemed to me the greatest cruelty not to see him as I knew him one last time, I backed away from his bedside. At the end of the bed I looked again, my final look, and saw that it was still that same unrecognizable face, not Peter at all, not the man I had known. I stumbled out of the room. There was a Catholic church next door to the hospital; I went straight there, on the way passing the priest who stood in the stillness and heat of the late afternoon washing his car. "Is the church locked?" I asked him, not pausing, as if I had been passing by and thought to drop in. "No," he said. "Go right in." He began to swab his car with a sponge or a bunched-up cloth while at his feet the hose trickled tepid water across the sun-heated gravel. I hated the moment, the way the orange sun spread itself across the dusty grass and the rough driveway; I hated the bleached sky, what I could see of it behind the high cross on the church roof; I hated the very feel of the parched air.

Inside the church the air was more alive and somehow fresher. I sat in a pew near the middle, off to one side. I don't know, now, why I didn't go to kneel at the altar. I suppose because I haven't been religious for many years. I sat alone only a few minutes when the priest came in and began to putter around at the back; I suppose he was making himself unobtrusively available to me, but instead of turning to him, I remember wishing he hadn't come in. I sat for a few more minutes, during which I felt only emptiness, a suspension of thought and feeling. I became very aware of the church's interior and the depth at the altar. Then I walked back to the hospital to begin, with his family, the business of Peter's death.

That late afternoon when Peter died, my older sister and her husband were already on their way from their home in British Columbia, landing at Medicine Hat in the early evening and renting a car to drive the 220 kilometres to our place. They would not arrive in Eastend until about 10 p.m., and as they didn't know the way, I was to meet them in town and lead them down the unmarked roads and through the rural darkness to the hay farm. I had at least three hours until then. While I waited, having no other idea of what to do to pass the time, trying to outrun the wall of emotion I feared would overcome me if I gave it room, I got down on my knees and washed the kitchen floor, all the while saying to myself, "My husband is dead; my husband is dead," as if by rehearsing this I might be able finally to believe it. I brought my family back to a spotless kitchen floor.

Over the months that followed Peter's death, we sold all his machinery and equipment and other items we had shared in our many years together. I said good-bye to the old broken snowmobile — recalling the night in a lull in the middle of a five-day blizzard we rode over eight-foot drifts to a neighbour's for coffee, and the time he rescued an old rancher post-storm on it — good-bye to the bicycles we'd ridden slowly down the lane on a summer evening, the horses, the various old trucks. It was good-bye to old furniture stored in this shed or that, things that were there when we married in 1976, all the possessions he had cleared out from the ranch when it was no longer ours, things that had belonged to his family going back to the early part of the twentieth century. I grew sadder, but I shed no tears. I seemed to be frozen.

After the funeral and the departure of my three sisters and their husbands and many friends as well as a few strangers, the months slowly passed. Finally, with the disposal of so many years' accumulation of things both useless and useful having been accomplished, including the machinery and equipment, and with the date of my leaving set, I was left alone on the place where I'd spent half my life. Each square of grass where trucks and implements had sat was deserted now, as were the sheds and shops; even the gates of the corrals gaped open, empty of animals. The entire place seemed to me to have a forsaken air, Quonset doors wide open on emptiness, feeders upended in the corrals, my footsteps echoing hollowly when I walked through the vacant outbuildings. My shoes would scrape pebbles or scuff up dust as I walked, the sound unnaturally loud and yet minuscule in the sudden wideness and emptiness of what had been the coziness of home. I had only to pack a few personal items and to make my final farewell.

It seemed to me, in those days, that the landscape faded, that the sky had retreated even farther away than usual and lost colour, and that the fields and hills had grown monochromatic, a uniform faded buff, as if the rocks and shrubs, the stone flakes and circles that lay scattered beside the Aboriginal cairns and graves, all of which I had known so well, had filled themselves in. It was as if the land had sealed itself away again, was no longer one where I might find history rising up to meet me. It had grown distant and silent, as it had been when, many years earlier, I arrived as a bride.

Every time I looked out the windows to the north and nothing out there spoke to me, the light no longer caught a boulder and gleamed unexpectedly, shadows no longer moved and paused for me, a lump would come into my throat and my chest would ache. In the days after all the work was done and the yard and fields were empty, slowly, I saw nature saying good-bye to me. It knew as well as I did, and my neighbours and my friends, that I was leaving the countryside and my life as a country woman for good. That I would not be back, that it — that life that had been mine — was over.

One morning a coyote came through the yard. This was a healthy animal, not mangy, or young and on its own for the first time, or wounded as wild animals coming into a farmyard in full daylight tend to be. This was a large, mature animal of the kind you saw only in the distance in fields as it was out hunting and you had ridden inadvertently into its range while checking cattle. It nosed its way under the pole fence that separated the yard from the narrow dirt road that ran more or less parallel to it, that before the sale had contained haying implements but that was now only a bare patch of trampled grass. Its thick fur was a glossy mix of dull gold and grey as it came trotting on a diagonal across the stiff ochre grass, past the leafless caraganas and the rough grey poplars and on down the gravel road that ran between the feed yard and house toward the barn and corrals at the bottom of the yard, and behind and below them where I could not see it, to the river crossing, where the water burbled softly over smooth-worn brown and grey stones, whispering its swift but delicate way through the broken, drowned grass. I watched from first one kitchen window and then another as the coyote moved by, oblivious to me. As I watched, I had a sense that the wild knew that I was the last living person here and that I would soon be gone. Otherwise, the coyote would not have come by so casually but so purposefully. It was as if I had already left.

Then, a day or so later, I heard the crunching of gravel and, thinking a truck was driving slowly into the yard, looked to see who it was. Trotting unhurriedly through the open gate was a massive male mule deer, his rack huge, the muscled flesh of his chest and haunches moving as he perambulated, sure of his own safety, proud as an emperor, his hooves striking the thinly spread gravel with an authoritative ring and clink. I watched him, not breathing as he moved on past the window at the end of the kitchen, as he went on down to the bottom of the yard and then, barely hesitating, veered to his left through the open gate into the second-to-last corral. Here he changed course again, to his right this time, and with the same stately, deliberate gait disappeared on his way down to the river. Such an extraordinary thing, I had never seen this before, an animal trotting down the yard as if the place were already gone back to the wild.

I had only a few days left now. There began to be a strange noise in the trees across the yard. I went out to stand on the deck, trying to see which tree it was coming from and what was making it. I deciphered the dark silhouette of a large creature sitting on a high branch in the tree on the far side of the lane that led through the yard down to the barn and corrals. It was framed by foliage and it was so big that for a moment I thought it was a cougar. But then it shifted slightly, changing its silhouette, and I saw that it was an enormous owl. As I watched, the bird lowered its head into its shoulders, then pushed it forward and emitted a sound like the single harsh bark of a dog. It did this again and again, the lowering of the head, the bark, and then again. Then I saw a second, equally large owl in a tree across the lane from the first and closer to where I stood watching from the deck. I had never before heard an owl make that noise, although I have read that there is one that does, but its range is far south of us in the United

States. One spring an owl had built its nest in the same trees and gave birth to and raised its owlets there, but never had it or its partner, coming and going with food, or the babes, made such a sound. I went slowly, filled with wonder, even a little frightened, back into the house.

After that, the owls were in those two trees, one on each side of the lane, every single day. There was no comforting familiar hooting: only that menacing movement and that bark, over and over and over again. I was counting down the days left to me: five, four, three, two. I think part of the reason I had been so wary of this pair, aside from the steady, strange bark of one of them, was that years before I had had a dream in which, as I walked across a field toward our home to the right, far ahead and deep in the valley, a giant black dog was bounding toward me across the fields ahead of me and on my left. It was one of those dreams that so terrify you there really is no way of conveying the intensity of the fear — fear that, surprisingly, didn't wake me as such dreams usually do at the last possible second when death is certain: the drowning, the fall off the cliff, the rapist, the man with the gun. This great black dog, murderous, implacable, was about to tear open my throat, to toss me and kill me. I was weaponless and alone, frozen in fear, in an instant would be torn apart. But just as the dog leaped upon me, in a flash that was a physical jerk to my eyes, at the last possible second, the dog vanished, having turned precisely into three dark-grey owls sitting side by side on the ground on my right and ahead of me. But the owls were also terrifying and, by the way they kept jumping up and by the vicious snapping of their beaks, as rapacious. How to get by them? As it happened, I was carrying a package of meat from the deep freeze, still wrapped in frost-covered, shiny tinfoil. I threw the package to the three owls; they dived upon it and began tearing it apart, forgetting me. I walked tentatively on past them toward the hay farm to the right and ahead of me, down in the cleft of the valley. *Then* I woke.

Now I see that dream as a warning and a prophecy of an immensely troubled time in my life that lay ahead of me, although I had no idea then about it, except to see it as a nightmare, more powerful than any other nightmare I had ever had. This nightmare didn't wake me at the point where I was to be killed so that I could dismiss it in daylight, but woke me only when I had overcome the danger, and was going on my way, slowly, home. That is why I am inclined to see it as a prophecy, or some serious statement about my life.

No wonder, then, that when the two owls appeared in the trees and behaved so strangely they loomed a good deal larger than they might have had Peter been standing beside me with his field glasses and the two of us with years ahead together. Under the circumstances, I couldn't help but take their presence as meaningful: nature, once again and in the most final way, acknowledging that it was time for me to go from that place. A day or two later, when I was cutting meat to make a stew, I deliberated for a while on all of this, not wanting to make whatever it was I was so afraid of worse. In the end, having no pets left to feed the scraps to, I took the trimmings from the meat — fat and gristle, a little bone — found the tinfoil wrapping paper we sometimes used for meat in the freezer, placed them in it, took the package outside, and placed it on the graveled lane between the two trees where the giant owls sat watching me. Then I went back inside, worrying that perhaps it wasn't wise to try to appease the world of dreams by a concrete action in the waking world. But now that it is 2015 and I am an older woman, the consideration of my passage through the world having become my very job, it seems to me a not unreasonable thing to have done.

When I went out to check some time later, the meat was gone, and so were the owls. In another day — the very next day — I too would be gone. When the time came, I drove away with no one to bid good-bye to; I drove away from no one at all, the tires of my

SUV crackling on the gravel, trailing shadows, memories, sorrows too immense to be recognized or delineated. It was late October 2008, and I was now sixty-eight years old.

The night Sean, my son, now a grown man with a job in Calgary and a wife and two beloved children, brought down a truck that was to be filled with a few bits of furniture and remaining items, a married couple who were friends came to help me pack. When they arrived, I had in each room one or two half-filled, open cardboard boxes. The wife came and asked me, as I worked in a bedroom, if she should close and tape the open boxes, and I could not even answer her, didn't know the answer, so without my response she went away, threw into the boxes the things she guessed I might want from each room, taped the boxes closed, and loaded them into the truck my son was filling with the small armchair Peter had given me for my birthday, a couple of lamps, a few basic kitchen items, some bedding, and some household tools. All this while I — did what? I'm not sure I did anything, although I was walking around looking at things without being able to make a single decision about so much as my toothbrush. I wonder now how on earth I thought I could manage the city. Perhaps by closing my eyes and leaping as I had done when, half a lifetime before, I left the city for my new life with Peter on the land.

I didn't know where or how I wanted to live in the world. I somehow believed an anvil would come crashing down from the sky with the name of the place I was supposed to be still smoking on it. It seemed far too early to think of buying a house or a condo. Besides the uncertainty that I was even in the right city, I found I could not cope with the simplest demand. I who had been an active rancher's wife and a busy writer and speaker seemed adrift. For two

years, then, I lived in a rented dingy one-bedroom apartment not
far from my son and his family, having arranged things so that all
I had to do was to write one cheque each month; it was all I could
manage. If I saw documents that required anything more, I started
to shake; I had to put them down and go into another room. It
might take me as long as three days before I could read and properly
digest what was in them, much less act on them. I can say about
this only that I was still in shock from the trauma of having to leave
behind everything I had cared about; I often felt (not without some
shame, given that it is so much worse for others) that I was like a
refugee who, overnight, has to abandon her home and community
for a strange country where she knows no one and does not even
speak the language.

In our life together Peter had been in charge of just about everything but the kitchen, and I had acquiesced in this chiefly because I
was not a rural person; I knew nothing about farming or ranching
or domestic animals other than pets. The ranch and the hay farm
were his; he handled the accounts and made all the decisions about
them, and his obvious competence meant that I would not have
thought of questioning him. I understood that his having married
at forty-one, years earlier having settled comfortably into his role
as owner and manager, meant that he would not be able to share
with me the running of the operation. I had thought — because
I was ignorant of that world, and in any case, did not want the
responsibility — this was wise. After all, over the years, I had created my own world as a writer next to his, and he did not intervene
in it.

With his death, I suddenly found myself in charge of everything. I did not even know which cheque-book to use or from
which account to pay simple household bills, and I was plunged
into managing the most intimate and important matters landown-
ers and householders in Canada have to deal with. I suppose that
what was wrong with me might have been diagnosed if I had sought

out a grief counselor. But my pride would not allow it. I see now how foolish that was. A part of it was probably my subconscious but powerful resistance to being alone, my rage at having to care for myself entirely. But looking back, I believe I was also trying to create a safe place for myself in which to heal before I ventured out to make my new life.

For two long years in the city, I stumbled around trying to make a life for myself, living in that small, dark apartment so that friends (the same friends who had helped me pack, or rather, who had packed for me) would say in dismay when they visited, "You should be living in a better place than this." Eventually, fate intervened. Well into my second winter in Calgary, there was an invasion of mice that even two different exterminators couldn't rid me of. I like to think now that Peter sent them, knowing as he did that if neither earthquake, avalanche, nor six-alarm fire, nor the drugged-out man I stepped over one morning to get into the parking garage could make me move again, a horde of mice could.

Or perhaps I was, at last, healing. With my son's constant help in showing me how to navigate the traffic, where certain stores were, and how urban people did things, I was getting used to the way people live in cities, and I was less frightened of my new environment. And as time passed, my grief mercifully started to lessen. Time can be a gift; it can blunt the worst of trauma and provide the sufferer some emotional distance from it. Somewhere around the time I moved into the sunny, two-bedroom condo I now live in as owner, I re-considered that ten-years-left notion. I'd been counting down the years ever since Peter died, watching without alarm but with disbelief as each one went by, and I was around the seven-years-left mark when one morning I woke and a voice said in my head, *Not ten years left; you have twenty left.* It sounded so authoritative that I didn't even think to dispute it. Besides, I knew the statistics by then. I was in good health; I probably would live about another fifteen to seventeen years.

Seventeen years! What a long time that is, I thought, so long that one can't really quite imagine it, and all my horizons deepened and dissolved into a fine mauve-coloured mist, as if I were thirteen again and had uncountable time before me. But with the possibility of a renewed life came the notion that it was too long, too much time. I didn't know how I would fill it beyond lunching with friends; going to movies, concerts, and plays. Worse, in the middle of a sleepless night it occurred to me that with so much time ahead of me I would live another life, a different life, that those thirty-three profound, sometimes magical years would be displaced. When I thought of that, I was aghast. And yet, as a writer I was quite able to imagine all sorts of twists and turns in the lives of my characters. Why should I be any different?

Nevertheless, until I was well into the writing that preceded the actual creation of this book, I was unable to remember a puzzling thing my mother once said to me. She died three days before her seventy-seventh birthday, when I was forty-six, of breast cancer, her second round with it, the whole business taking four years from the beginning when in the shower she found a lump in one breast while visiting her younger sister Jessie in Florida — she who had never had the chance to travel — telling no one, deciding it could wait until she got home a month later, to the end.

This was in the week before she drew her last breath as she lay in bed at the house of one of my sisters in Saskatoon, and the day before she fell into the three-day coma that would end with her death. I must have been wanting to have that last mother-daughter conversation that would explain everything to me about my life, her life, our family's life, and knowing she would soon be gone and that I could never again ask her a question, I leaned over her, waiting for her to open her eyes. Private mother-daughter conversations are scarce in a family of five girls; there was too much competition for her time and she had had so little of it when we were all at home driving her crazy with all our demands and needs.

Everybody else was for the moment downstairs, washing dishes, getting a breath of fresh air, crying quietly in the bathroom. It was my moment.

I don't know where the question came from. I know I had not framed it exactly, although I will acknowledge that I wanted to ask her something about her life, or what she thought about life in general now, at this decisive moment. Perhaps I wanted some word from her that would change my own life.

"Mom," I said, as gently as I could, and softly, so as not to startle her, "when was the best time?" I meant the best period of her life, knowing that she had always made us think of our family's beginnings in the bush wilderness of northeast Saskatchewan as the worst possible time, and knowing also that she had already had her great life dream, the one that is viewed by those who work with the dying as a significant marker of impending death — an idyllic picture of herself on horseback galloping across a flower-dappled, sunshine-bathed green meadow. The image came out of her girlhood on the Manitoba prairie, where she had been born; I remembered her telling us when we were little girls, her eyes distant, her face glowing, "There is nothing like galloping on a horse, your hair streaming out behind, things rushing by you, the power of the horse under you. . . ." Maybe she was going to repeat *that* story again. Or maybe it would be, "When you were all little girls around me and your father and I . . ." (Our father, who had died at only sixty-seven, had been dead for fourteen years.) Or maybe her teen years in the 1920s, when she appeared in the small black-and-white photos of the time to have a ton of girlfriends, all laughing together and acting silly. Or maybe in mid-life, when we were gone from home and she got a job and had her own money and was out in the adult world again.

Moistening her lips with her tongue, her jaw moving for just a second before she could make a sound, startling me by lifting a thin hand — what small, beautiful hands our mother had — to point shakily down toward her chest, in a voice I had to lean closer to hear, she said, as emphatically as she could manage, "Now!"

If I was staggered by this, and I must have been, there was so much more to think about just then: the palliative nurse's daily visit, questioning the doctor about this or that — medication, management, that sort of thing — our own memories, our own lives on hold for this terrible week, our own children coming and going, friends and relatives phoning. Strangely, I don't remember thinking about what she said again until I decided years later to write this book. I was well into my research, reading books about aging, writing reams and reams that would all hit the paper shredder or the recycling bin, when suddenly I remembered.

With growing awe and surprise, I remembered that she had chosen her old age as the best time of her life, had chosen it even while she was about to die, when surely we at last encounter the truth, when we no longer have any reason to prevaricate. With our father dead, all of us grown and scattered across the western provinces, she was living alone in a small house in an older, tree-lined district of the city, growing beautiful flowers in her small backyard, reading huge amounts of not-too-demanding literature (she especially liked historical fiction). This very smart woman chose a simple existence, even turning down a marriage offer from an old family friend without seeming to give it the smallest consideration, as if she had had enough of *real* life, watching television, knitting and embroidering, visiting occasionally with friends, relatives from elsewhere dropping in as they passed through town, her social life reduced to family gatherings with her children, their spouses, and her grandchildren if they could be rounded up to attend. She was alone a lot, especially in winter, but she never complained. She was calm and exuded an air of peacefulness, no longer seemed discontented or angry, but ruminated about her past as she knitted or hooked a small rug. Gentleness had entered her demeanour, and most interesting of all was the way, over those last few years, she had become beautiful. I see this only now, from a perspective of twenty-seven years without her, but I think all of this might have been a kind of happiness.

How odd it was that I didn't recall this moment. That such a time in her life might be the best was inconceivable to me then, and in a mixture of bafflement and disbelief, I filed her reply to my question somewhere deep, wishing she had never said it. I still wanted to believe that life — anybody's life — held some kind of dramatic pay-off. But the older I get, the more I wonder at the way the human memory works: Everything is there, stored away, waiting for the right moment to come rushing back into consciousness. Now I was old and widowed myself, in a time when the inescapable realization that I would never again be young had arrived, when I was invisible on the street and in stores and cafés. I, who had spent my mid-life, well over thirty years, in the midst of vast acres of wild grass, was now living the truncated life of the urban condo dweller, alone. *This*, I thought, *this* was my mother's best time of her life? When she was alone?

Stranded in the alien kingdom of the city, loneliness and fear alternating with exhilaration and hopefulness, I pondered this mystery.

2

THE LOW HORIZON

Sharon walking at the ranch circa 1995.

3

The Great Leap

I first saw the southwest in about 1974, and it felt to me as if I had come into another country and different, earlier century to live. I asked myself how I could have lived in Saskatchewan almost all my life and not even known this place existed. Although the area I'm writing about is bigger than the state of Vermont, there are few highways leading into or through it; no wide, swiftly flowing rivers; no majestic lakes or snow-capped purple mountains or even cities to attract visitors, nor is it a route to something exciting just over the border in the United States. Farms, ranches, graveled roads leading to small towns, villages, and hamlets are set in a vast (then) relatively untouched landscape. With the exception of the beautiful Cypress Hills and the interprovincial park that runs east–west across the bulk of the hills, there seemed to be no reason at all to go there.

When I first saw it, the entire region — excluding the small city of Swift Current — had a population of only about 10,000 people: Vermont's population is about 700,000. Or, if you prefer, the smaller area I went to live in is about five times bigger than Prince Edward Island, which has a population of about 147,000. In fact, the region where the ranch is located went from having no stable, resident Euro-Canadian population in the 1880s to a slow influx of settlers until, in the twenties, it reached a population of about twenty per square mile (that is, there was either a single male or a family on nearly every quarter section), but by the time I arrived, in the seventies, this was reduced to about 1.5 persons per square mile. This meant that in practice there were many large areas on which nobody at all lived; for the most part, these areas are still unpopulated. The ranch when I first arrived was then about twenty square miles — four miles by five miles — in size, but it was bordered on the west and north by a provincial pasture of about one hundred square miles in size. On these two pieces of land lived only the Butala family, and perhaps six miles away, the pasture manager and his family on the provincial government pasture. The other closest homes were each about four miles from the Butala house to the south, southeast, and east.

The particular area where the Butala ranch is located wasn't opened for settlement until about 1910, when all the best land and land closest to established towns of some size and to the railway had already been taken. Those who adapted best were those who accepted that nobody could survive on a mere 160 acres, as the land wasn't fertile enough; that at least 640 acres or a full section, one mile by one mile, was the basic amount needed; and further, given the quality of the soil, that ranching was probably a better plan than farming. The eventually more than 13,000 acres of the Butala ranch had at one time been the small holdings of something like eighteen families or single men; these people, one by one, had left, only a dozen or so actually acquiring title to their land before they gave up and moved elsewhere. Some parts of the ranch had never had a single settler on them.

Over one hundred years since the opening for settlement, southwest Saskatchewan is still a thinly populated area and, despite all the certainty of various villages that one day they would be metropolises, it still does not have a single large city. Today the farms in the province have an average size of 1,668 acres — that is, almost three sections per family or corporation. People with that much land, given the current weather and improved agricultural practices, usually do very well. Nowadays, with the demise of the Wheat Board and the provincial wheat pools and the single-desk marketing system, this over the protests of the majority of farmers, as it puts business interests over those of the ordinary people who work the land, every farmer is pretty much on his own when it comes to selling his crops, and if he isn't good with figures and computers, he doesn't survive. Not only are there far fewer farms than before, but most of the open prairie, where plowing is a good deal easier than in forested lands where the tree stumps and roots have to be removed first, has been worked, changing the nature of the land forever.

It clearly hadn't occurred to Peter that he might be asking too much of me — trying to turn a non-agricultural person whose favourite field was the arts rather than wheat or hay, into a rural woman — and I had assumed that I would get along: I would make good friends; I would participate; I would enjoy myself; I would trade in the rigorous life of the single-parent, working woman in the intensely competitive world of the university, for life as a ranch woman. We were, both of us, completely out of our minds, and everybody could see that but us. At thirty-six and forty-one, respectively, we didn't even have the excuse of being young.

We would, before our wedding, in a decision that was agony for me, allow Sean to stay in the city with his father. He had told me close to the time we were to move south how very much he didn't want to go. He didn't want to lose his friends or his coaches. He wanted to see his father regularly. I had had misgivings all along about putting a city child into the country milieu, and although I had custody, I gave in. How many women have had to make that heart-rending choice, between their adolescent children and a chance at a new, satisfying life? I did not think I was making that choice, though. Our agreement was that all long weekends and holidays, including summer, he would spend with me.

In the end, living without him was almost too hard. If I hadn't known how well he was doing in school and in his sports activities, and how happy he seemed to be in his new home, I don't think I would have lasted with Peter; I would have had to go back to the city.

Some feminist theorists argue that to place the moral/ethical burden of such choices on just the mother is unfair. All I know is what I felt in my heart: a nagging guilt at leaving my son, even though he was happy.

Imagine my first sight of Eastend: driving into the village of six hundred or so at dusk on a muddy Victoria Day weekend, to find a puzzlingly wide main street, on each side of which was a row of Western-style false-fronted small frame shops and cafés; I would learn to call the cafés Jack's and Charlie's and would never go into Charlie's, as it was then frequented by men only, although on a sweltering summer day if I happened to be in town I might reach up from the sidewalk to buy a soft ice cream cone from its side window. On each side of the main block of the street, half-tons were parked nose-in, one after the other, with stock racks on their boxes, many with the motors running, so that clouds of pink-purple exhaust rose into the luminous sapphire of the evening, and the soft rumbling of the motors was (before everyone knew about global warming and climate change) a comforting, homey sound.

I had arrived in a TR4 sports car driven by a professor of, as I recall, biology — his work involved the University of Saskatchewan's electron microscope, one of the few then in the world and the size of a room (today most of them are merely desktop-size instruments) — with my twelve-year-old son squeezed into the tight area behind us. We had come to see the ranch, owned and run by my "cousin" (we'd always referred to the family there as cousins, although my four sisters and I had never met them, and their relationship to us was distant), who had invited us. Or rather, we were invited by my forty-year-old bachelor cousin Peter, who owned and ran the family ranch started by his father and two uncles in the early part of the century and who wanted the chance to show it off to me.

If it had been up to me I'd never have gone — what, me? A ranch? Why would I want to go to a ranch? But the professor and my son were both keen to go, Sean in particular jumping with eagerness to see a cattle ranch and real cowboys. The professor, who was from the British Isles, offered to drive us in return for the chance to see a real Canadian cattle ranch too. So I succumbed and off we went, on the wrong weekend, so that we weren't expected, and when we arrived, we had some trouble locating our hapless host.

To get to the ranch from Saskatoon, where both the professor and I taught at the University of Saskatchewan and he did research of some mysterious variety, you turned south at Rosetown, seventy miles west of Saskatoon, onto Highway 4 and kept going south for about 150 miles and then turned west, and eventually south for another maybe fifty miles before you went the last ten miles west again, and there you were, about fifteen miles north of the Montana border and about thirty from the Alberta border to the west: precisely in the middle of nowhere. Even today, with the advent of serious oil and gas exploration and extraction, a cyclic business if ever there was one, the ranch is still in the middle of precisely nowhere. That is, if by *nowhere* you mean acres and acres and acres with nobody living on it, no houses, no stores, no bars (as might be found if you were in Montana, where a mere crossroads might, in those days, have as many as four bars parked, one on each of its corners, despite there not being a single ranch or farmhouse in evidence anywhere near), and almost no traffic. A whole day might go by without a single vehicle passing on the sparsely graveled dirt road that ran past the buildings, and I can attest to this, as I would eventually spend many days there, mostly alone, watching for the single half-ton churning up a fat worm of yellow dust as it whined by, before the particles rose into a choking cloud, then thinned, and dissipated into the blue.

But on that particular wrong weekend, we were heading for the hay farm, not the ranch. In fact, it was Peter who had made the mistake, and we discovered that when — this was pre–cell phones — we found a pay phone and reached him as he and his friends were taking a coffee break in the log house and thus, luckily, he heard the phone ringing. He said, "I did mean the twenty-fourth of May weekend, but I thought it was next week."

"No," I pointed out. "This is the long weekend. It's early this year." Of course, with our jobs and school for my son, and the distance involved, we couldn't have come on any but a long weekend. I think he was laughing then, and gave us instructions on how to reach the hay farm where he was, about ten miles southeast of Eastend. The instructions were, typically for Peter, casual as opposed to exact, but we didn't know that then. It was a cold, rainy, windy weekend, but because of the ample spring rains that year, the landscape was intensely green. Although the road out of town — in those days a graveled, curving, uphill run between a dirt cliffside with a steep drop on the other side until you reached the plateau above the Frenchman River valley at the bottom of which the town was set — was wet, it was well enough graveled so as not to cause us serious trouble in our little car. It wasn't until we hit the mile of dirt road on the Butala land that followed the river into the house yard (as opposed to the feed yard or the barnyard), that the professor required every ounce of his strength to hold the wheel where he wanted it, and all his skill as a driver to keep the car straight and moving ahead.

The road was pure gumbo, a term that hadn't meant much to me before I started driving around in the southwest. Gumbo is wet clay, and people were always joking that you had to drive in it because you couldn't walk in it. You often couldn't even stand up in it, it was as slippery as wet soap, and if you drove, your vehicle would sink in; it would gum up your wheels and fill the wheel wells until your vehicle came to a full stop and couldn't move. That's what happened to us. We had to struggle the rest of the way in to the house through the wind and rain, and later Peter and the professor would go out in a tractor and pull the car in. It was not the last time in the years I lived there that I would have to give up, get out, slam the truck door shut, and walk in.

I would eventually learn that the only way to drive the gumbo roads without getting hopelessly stuck was to point your vehicle in the direction you wanted to go, put your foot pretty hard on the gas, and neither deviate in your course nor let up on the gas until you got to where you were trying to go. Only men, in those days, drove those roads in wet weather; it was the rare woman who would even try. Mothers, particularly, were afraid to have accidents that would hurt their children or render themselves incapable of looking after them. Not to mention that husbands tended to yell if they had to stop their work to pull you out of a ditch, or if you put dents in their vehicles. In this, Peter was a definite exception. He didn't even make sarcastic remarks, or mutter *sotto voce* as he dragged out chains and put the heavy iron hooks on the axle or frame (never the bumper) or wrapped the chains around it. I only ever heard him yell at a horse once, and that was to make it stop as it raced, riderless, for an open gate. When he was in a confrontation with a neighbour who had a strong tendency to violence in order to clarify his opinions, Peter's voice got softer, more conversational. The discussion was, of course, as any country person already knows, about fences.

It turned out that the road we tried to drive down that day more than forty years ago wasn't even a real road. I would find that out in later years, when I had grown to love the very dirt of it and the way it meandered carelessly along the river's edge and where all one summer I watched a pair of giant owls nesting on the crumbling cliffside right below it, having learned that owls tended not to notice you if you were quiet enough, and peered over the edge down at them as they bobbled around, companionably making a nest. The "road" was merely a trail scraped out by the PFRA, referred to by everybody as "the PF." PFRA stands for Prairie Farm Rehabilitation Administration, a federal agency inaugurated in 1935 to help prairie farmers, some of whom were literally starving to death, as were their cattle and horses, with no crops to sell, their land blowing away, no rain for years, and, although it was cold in winter, hardly any snow either. In those grim days, farming practices were not yet sophisticated enough to allow for the conservation of soil and moisture. "The PF" was an odd-sounding name, I suppose, but perfectly reasonable to prairie people, and trailing a long, unspoken, and unhappy history. So the "road" we got stuck on that day was a PF trail, and part of the hay farm was part of the PF project.

In fact, the entire valley in which the hay farm was situated and through which the small river ran from the PF dam at the western edge of town (the river started in the Cypress Hills and for the first years of settlement had been called the White Mud for the high-quality clay outcroppings along its banks), all the way to the town of Val Marie, nearly a hundred miles east and south, was an intermittent series of PF irrigation projects. Peter and his family had owned their hay farm since Peter was fifteen, and had gone through years of intense labour with equipment of a kind I'd never heard of, to level it and dike it and create on the valley bottom eventually about two hundred acres of flood-irrigable hay land. The trail along the river that we got so completely stuck in late that day was only a truck-width narrow trail running along the edge of the river that the PFRA ditchriders used to check the way the water was running in the fields as they were irrigated, sometimes to change "sets," or to open and close headgates, and down which they could bring any needed machinery.

It turned out there was another road, one that bisected the land itself with actual gravel on it, a municipal road engineered to be higher than the ditches, but Peter had neglected to mention it. I'll never know if that was an accident or not, but he, like a lot of the other men of the area, liked people, especially city people, to know how bad the roads were. They wouldn't make it easy for you. The provincial government did so little for them then, probably because the entire area held at that time a paltry 10,000 votes in total (and they tended not to be for the political party that was in power, as the prevailing mind-set in the southwest was Alberta- or American style conservatism). They were quietly angry about this. They thought of themselves as men's men, tough and capable and unfazed by mere bad to impassable roads — hadn't their pioneering parents and grandparents braved much worse? They casually maneuvered what city people couldn't handle. They were implacably tough and capable, as I would learn. The men among whom I would spend thirty-three years were physically strong and had become that way through simply living their lives working with cattle and horses; they often wore ragged and stained clothing because they did physical labour all day, much of it with machinery, and they had, as I would learn, built the world in which they lived: the roads, the crops in the fields, the corrals, fences, the water wells, sometimes even the houses they lived in.

Even Peter's generation, born in 1934, understood the world as having started from the way nature made it — long sweeps of grass, hills, rocks, burnouts and hardpan, an occasional patch of shrubs — and having to be scraped and dug out and built upon by their grandfathers and fathers and by themselves. They did not recognize an already built world; perhaps did not even care for one.

I had come from such a world myself, but many years before, when I was a small child in the wilderness I had managed with ease to tuck it away in the far back of my brain, where I had intended never to bring it out again. The city, I was sure, was for me. Until I met Peter.

I think we ate supper that first night in Jack's Café, late at night, or it might be that we went to Peter's parents' house in town and his mother had supper, or at least a late lunch set out for us. I see flashes of this and that, remember a cowboy as we sat around at Peter's mother's house say something about not being "rarin' n' tearin' to go," at which the professor had to hide his laugh at such a quaint turn of phrase. A real cowboy turn of phrase, I guess it would have seemed to him, something he would never have heard in the UK. I remember, later that night, the stars; I thought I had never seen so many stars in my whole life crowded into one vast ink-dark sky, little flower-like clusters, single burning stars or planets, far and scattered pale bands of filmy white stars, and no other light at all except a sort of jury-rigged low yard light in front of the log house where we stayed, and in which Peter lived, that you had to switch on yourself before you went outside.

We spent all the next day watching the men work. It was skilled work they were doing; you couldn't just offer to help, because you had to be able to ride a horse, you had to be able to tell a steer from a cow or a bull, or indeed, a horse, and to recognize when to open a corral gate and when not to. It was all so strange to us that watching seemed the best bet, and it was so interesting that we didn't ever find ourselves bored. The professor, a talented amateur photographer (this before digital photography), walked around taking pictures all day, changing lenses occasionally, and getting what I

still think were some very good shots of my curly-haired boy cling-
ing for dear life to the hoof of a calf that was about to be branded;
me sitting on the high corral fence watching; the men roping, or
just riding along through the tall grass on the riverbank, laughing
together, one of them coiling his rope, another cupping his palm
around his mouth in just such a way as to make a call we'd never
heard before, neither a whistle, yodel, or shout, but a bit of a blend
of all three, while ahead of them cows plodded along, and calves
galloped their rocking-horse gait, and kicked up their heels in sheer
delight at the world.

Sometimes, when I think about that weekend as I do now, I
think it was infused with a kind of magic, although it is so easy to
use that word. It was otherworldly to the three of us, the greens
greener than we had seen before, the muted melody of the narrow river more musical than other running streams, the ease of
the men as if this were nothing at all, seated on their horses as if
they had been born there, the wine-red backs of the Hereford cattle
richly colourful against the grass and brownish-green water, even
the creaking of the long wooden gates as someone pushed one open
or dragged one shut telling us a new story. I was not cold, I was not
sorry I'd come or eager to leave. We had come down that long road,
driving for hours, and somehow, when I wasn't paying attention
and never expected it, had driven into another world.

By the time it was over and we were in that speedy, romantic
little car heading back to Saskatoon, I had parted ways with the
professor and declared myself to be Peter's — what? Girlfriend? I
blush even now, at seventy-five, to think of it. Although the professor, whom I recently ran into again, now a married man with
grown children and grandchildren, seems to have forgiven me. He
went on to have an exotic life, which can't be said of me, so perhaps
he had long ago forgotten my perfidy. Or maybe he was graciously
admitting that all is fair in war and love.

I can remember clearly the explanation of what was going on

in the corrals and why the animals were being brought in from the fields, sorted, and loaded into Peter's four-ton truck to be driven off elsewhere. I don't suppose it made much sense to me then, but it would become in time one of the two biggest events of our working year: In the late fall we would trail the cattle through the snow and cold from the far northeast corner of the ranch across frozen fields and down trails and roads to the hay farm in the valley, where we could look after them for the winter, and then — if things went as we wanted them to — we would trail them back again to the ranch for spring, summer, and fall. Each way was a three-day trek — usually during Christmas holidays so that Sean could take part — and required as many riders as we could snag and find horses for if they didn't have their own. As you might expect, it was easy to find a crew to chase the cattle back south in the spring; in the dead of winter between Christmas and New Year's to drive them north to the hay farm it was often impossible. More than once the crew consisted of Peter, me, and one old cowboy-rancher who drove the truck, and with whom Peter would confer occasionally as to how to solve a problem, or where the trail we were on broke and which way we should go. The knowledge, the wisdom of the old, despite the father-son battles over just about everything having to do with ranching, was greatly respected when I first went to the southwest to live. I loved that aspect of the culture, and regret that it has nearly vanished in cities, where the old are for the most part ignored, or treated by the young and sometimes even the middle-aged with a profound lack of respect.

But that spring when my son, the professor, and I arrived on the wrong weekend, it had rained and rained, so that Peter had held off trailing the cows to the ranch, hoping for better weather, until the moment had come when he had only maybe a day or two of feed left for them in the valley — that is, he was completely out of winter feed, and had no choice but to get them to the ranch as fast as possible, where there was both old and some new grass for them to eat. That meant rounding up a volunteer crew; chasing the cattle all in, not a very big job on only a section of land, sorting them — you wouldn't, for example, put the cows in a packed trailer with their calves, as the calves might be trampled or otherwise hurt — and taking them load by load nearly forty miles southwest by road back onto the ranch. It was, as Peter would explain to visitors who exclaimed over so much land, in Canada merely a medium-size ranch, although as far as I know, in the mid-seventies it was, I think, the biggest one in the local area. To us, completely new to the terrain and way of life, the size wasn't comprehensible. The ranch was nearly entirely native prairie, not flat land, as around Regina, the capital city, but low lazy hill after hill receding endlessly into the sky.

In later years, when all of this had been home to me for a long time, I sometimes used to take friends to the high highway that ran above the southern border of the ranch (with a few fields belonging to neighbours between the road we traveled east on and the south border), and drive slowly a couple of miles along it, urging my companions to look to the north.

"That is the ranch," I would say softly, not even bothering to point, and there would be an awed silence, or a breathless *ohhhh*. I never stopped feeling that wonder myself: miles of blue-green, pale yellow, or snow-covered white hills extending as far as the eye could see, and beyond Peter's land, all the way to the low horizon. It was like looking at a mythical, pre-contact Wyoming, a green Nunavut, a grassed Sahara. It put your heart up into your mouth.

My relationship to it was fragile, though, and that is why I never gazed at it comfortably as an owner does. I was Peter's wife, my name went on the titles (eventually), but I had not discovered it, settled it, filled it with cattle, raised children on it, nor been a child raised on it, and in the face of all that, my mere title of "wife" wasn't worth much to anybody. I would never be an equal to Peter or to any of his family members, although in the end I rivalled even his siblings in the number of years I was an "owner" there. Even his mother, who actually lived on the place from about 1934 on into the mid-sixties, when Peter's father's ill health drove his parents into town, put in the same number of years as I did. Of course, she lived on the ranch full-time for all those years while Peter and I, once we built the new house in the valley, lived there only sporadically, only summers, and otherwise when we were working there.

No, I cannot honestly say I ever felt like an owner of that place. I had the tenuous status of the daughter-in-law who comes from another family. In rural families, where everything is about land and land ownership, whoever marries the son has taken on rights she didn't earn as the family members did. She doesn't have a birthright as they do. She will never be fully a member of that family. In my years there, that would in the end stretch to thirty-three on the hay farm and partly on the ranch, I never felt a rock-solid sense that I had a right to be there, that the place was mine too. And yet, it was my home; I had no other home.

I had some trouble seeing this at the time, although now, from my new perspective in the city, it is perfectly clear. How hard it must be for the women of any land-owning family who will not inherit land and will have to leave, often for the city or town or for some other family's land, to see their birthright become another woman's. Until the time comes when the old British system of the land going to the eldest son as a way of keeping wealth together is deposed so that each child regardless of gender receives an equal share, this burden will continue for the women of most rural agricultural land-holding families.

That weekend when I first saw the place, I rode with Peter in his rattling old four-ton truck loaded with cattle all the way to the ranch, which he always referred to as being forty miles from the hay farm, and by which he meant house to house; watched him back up to the sloped dirt loading ramp, the earth held in place with stout vertical planks, and let the cattle out; watched them disperse before he put the truck back into gear and we headed back to the hay farm to get another load. I knew he was happy; on the way back to the hay farm he didn't brake going down the hills as he would always do otherwise, especially in a vehicle like that one — big and rickety — but let us sail down them as if we were flying. I sensed that buoyancy was what he felt in his heart that day. I remembered that the first time we had seen each other in the city his eyes, a light blue, had darkened and taken on a glitter as he gazed at me, a look that would have frightened me in a stranger. Being a girl of a certain era, I saw it for what it was; I tossed my head like a beauty queen. This was months before I saw him again, when my son, the professor, and I drove south and found him in the midst of rounding up and trucking cattle from hay farm to ranch.

I have written in my 1994 memoir, *The Perfection of the Morning: An Apprenticeship in Nature*, what I felt when I first saw the land of the southwest opening before me; I'd come from a city and from a university community where we didn't look up into the sky much unless we were astronomers or studying the aurora borealis (as my first love back in 1958 had done). Mostly we looked at each other and at street signs and buildings; we strode hallways and classrooms, rarely the wilderness. We thought, like so many people, that if you hadn't hiked the Himalayas and you hadn't trekked through the Nahanni or the Serengeti, you hadn't seen nature, as if nature were some very rare commodity, available only to the most daring and wealthiest.

Bookstores were beginning to fill with books about where nature was (across the ocean, at the top of mountains, in the midst of vast deserts, in the jungles of hot continents), with the how-tos containing practical suggestions for finding potable water, crossing a bridgeless river, greeting strange new tribes. There were exciting and/or ecstatic memoirs of such trips. Before too many years had passed, I began to wonder if humankind had lost its mind. Wasn't the ant crawling along the house foundation nature? Wasn't the vegetable garden in the backyard? Wasn't the uncut field? Even what lived at the garbage dump? The foxes, badgers, and skunks that ran in the ditches along the roads, the insects and mice in the cracks in the sidewalks, the birds perched on high ledges and rooflines, the clever raccoons rummaging in urban garbage cans, and the coyotes stalking small dogs in suburban yards?

There began to be, in those early years, a growing interest in the spiritual in nature, and also in the knowledge of such matters that Aboriginal people held — the elders in particular. Carlos Castaneda was in full flight, read with held breath by millions, me included, and to this day no one is sure if he was purely a charlatan or a true visionary — perhaps he was a little of both. The North American world, after generations of building cities and touting them — fully believing in them — as the best solution to the ills of humankind, now was beginning to yearn for the more natural world that had been lost through the industrial revolution, through fossil-fueled industries and transportation modes, and in the ranks of shining city towers, the rubble-strewn ghettos, the regimented, too-tidy, clock-driven suburban world.

That was the very time I found Peter and the ranch.

Indeed, the chief gift of my new life turned out to be living in nature: Peter and I lying in bed on a summer night with all the windows open and hearing the hissing snarl only feet away of a passing bobcat, or maybe it was a lynx, or even a cougar, and then, as we froze and listened hard, hearing not another sound; at the hay farm Peter calling me softly to come and watch a small herd of elk appear against the skyline on the hills to the south as we stood at the door of the old log house gazing up, not moving; lying on our stomachs in the tall grass on a bank above a slough to see the wild swans on their migration north gliding back and forth on the dark water; hearing the first V of geese in the spring circling from the east or the west, honking, looking for water and feed, flying so low over us that we could hear the powerful beat of their wings as they captured air and pushed it away. It did something to you, as if your heart weren't in your chest anymore but was rising into the air with those great birds. More than once there were pelicans, it seemed to me the most skittish of the great birds, at least when they were in our country, and sometimes, rarely, a moose that had strayed too far south, and at the ranch there were always antelope skimming the hills in the distance, flowing in pale, dreamlike bunches over the fields. Deer were there, both mule and white tail, every morning and every evening. And coyotes, the most interested in humans, their signature songs background to the rising and setting of the sun. I got used to seeing golden eagles, hawks were everywhere, and in the spring or fall a lone bald eagle or a pair of them might pass by or roost in our trees for a day or so, or blue herons came, flapping their great wings in a leisurely, half-clumsy fashion, as if they had all the time in the world, and were lords of everything they saw. In winter, snowy owls, so eerie and beautiful, so purely white that they startled you as they suddenly rose up off a fence post as you passed by down the snow-covered trail.

It seemed a miracle to me that I had been fortunate enough to have found this nature-driven world to escape to.

4

A Map of the World

Having married Peter, I came to the southwest as a wife in the spring of 1976. The world I moved into was purely rural and nearly completely agricultural. This was long before the social mobility of thoroughly urban people who, believing in the possibility of some pastoral idyll, and often retired or prosperous enough not to need jobs, began to move in surprisingly large numbers to remote rural villages and towns where a liveable house was breathtakingly cheap and the cost of living much lower. An urban person in the community then was a rarity, aside from the current local doctor, maybe, or some of the teachers. I had not lived in such an environment since the day we left the last small town for the metropolis of Saskatoon when I was thirteen, and although both my parents came from farms, and I had visited my grandparents on their farm, I had never lived on one. In contrast, Peter had spent part of two winters in Saskatoon at agricultural school when he was about sixteen and seventeen, living in a dorm with a lot of other rural boys, and that was the sum total of his experience of urban life. As his mother once said of herself and her family, "We are as rural as you can be. Nobody is more rural than we are."

The whole area was more rural than it is today, and a good deal more insular, with little population drift in or out, except, as Peter told me, usually the "best" having left because there has been no-where to go here, no way to get ahead visibly and quickly, farming being too slow and always uncertain. Others said, "Anybody with any get-up-and-go got up and went," but I always found that interesting, because the speaker, not a failure, had stayed and didn't seem rancorous about it. So I felt they must have meant a particular personality type, someone eager for a faster-paced, more exciting, more peopled world, and with more sure money, maybe even a little glamour. It would be explained to me that in families where one person left for the city, that person always did better financially through his life than had the siblings who stayed behind to work at jobs in the villages or out on the land as farmers or ranchers. Young men might find it necessary for a few years to go off north to work in construction or in the oil fields or as ranch hands on one of the storied ranches in British Columbia, while they waited to take over the family land, but the younger generation rarely went away to get a higher education then. And a girl who didn't marry a local boy soon went away, and usually didn't come back, having no land to come back to.

There was thus a kind of purity about the place and the people in those days, whose culture depended utterly on land ownership, the handling of cattle herds, riding and managing horses, looking after grazing fields and farms with their crops to be marketed, with the weather and the seasons (then both perfectly predictable) and everyone knowing everyone else or related to one another. Everything was ordained by the land itself, and the community was a tight network of intense relationships. Here the best possible thing a woman could be was a nurse. A nurse was respected in that physical society because she knew what to do if someone lost an arm in a baler, or rolled a truck, or smashed a leg under a horse out in the field or at the rodeo, or if a baby ran a high fever, or a child got hit on the head and wouldn't wake up. This, of course, was because either there was no doctor at all nearby, or in the earliest days he might well be a little mad, an incompetent, an alcoholic or drug addict, or on the run from a bad mistake elsewhere, or else (if not both) trying to serve offices in a couple of villages and thus overly busy, and hard to catch up with. Not to mention the bad roads and the paucity or complete absence of ambulances. My college education, then, was fairly useless.

So I spent the first year almost constantly with Peter, in the field, in small towns waiting while he got parts, at elevators, in the café, on horseback, in the corrals, in cattle buyers' offices or at the sale ring, or crossing the land in a truck. Now and then, when there was a long stretch between holidays or long weekends, and I was missing Sean too much, I would drive to the city to see him, staying with my widowed mother and spending whatever time with him we could manage between his soccer games or his swim meets or other activities in his busy teenager's life. Often I would drive to the city to bring him "home" for a long weekend or Christmas or Easter vacations. Then we would have five hours together each way without anyone else, and our bond, never broken but sometimes stretched thinner through absence than I would have wished, would be renewed. And yet, although I wrestled with the worry every day, I couldn't bring myself to give up my marriage. How many women have gone through this pain? How many women never get over their guilt? I can say, however, that as might be expected, it got easier for both of us as Sean grew older and more independent.

By my new marriage, though, I had entered what was then in Saskatchewan the magical kingdom of the farm from which both of my parents had been displaced. I was learning also that I was a woman living within the great myth of the cowboy West. Both of these fascinated me, and I wanted to know all about them. But the second couldn't be asked about, could only be observed and considered. About the first, I never stopped asking questions, and Peter got great pleasure out of teaching me. Once we even took a cattle oiler apart: We sat on the truck's tailgate, parked out in a field miles from anywhere, and as the oiler has two arms, he took one of them apart piece by piece and I sat beside him imitating each step with the second arm. I don't remember what the problem was, but I know we fixed it. I felt immeasurably competent after that. I went with him in the half-ton to chase the horses into the corrals, a rough, exciting ride that was better than anything at the fair, and in the winter more than once on his dilapidated snowmobile when the road into the ranch was closed by snow and we had to get in to feed and check the horses and make sure that the house was all right. When the horses were elsewhere or in use or we were in a hurry, I rode with him on his motorcycle to check fields and cattle. I was often in the cab with him while he cut hay or baled it. When he moved loads from one place to another, I followed him in the truck. During this early period he was teaching me about the business of ranching, the daily chores, the seasonal rounds, the weather, the earth, the grass, the habits of horses and cattle, even of the wild animals and birds of the fields. I started to understand that the birds and the animals were the rural person's daily newspaper: the weather report, the news of seasonal changes, or news alerts when something went wrong.

The day finally arrived when Peter came from where he had been tinkering in the shop to the house to tell me he was going somewhere on an errand, assuming I would get my jacket and go with him, and I, thinking it was time I tried to map a world of my own as well as the one we had together, said, "Thanks, but I think I'll stay here this time." He was surprised, but if he was disappointed, he didn't show it. I think I just spoke first, that he was already thinking this way of operating, unusual as it was, couldn't go on forever.

That was when my wanderings began. That was when I began to explore my new environment, by myself, without Peter there to lead, show, and interpret. Like most twentieth-century North American adults, I'd spent most of my days indoors. The last office at the university I'd shared with one or two others had painted concrete-block walls and not even a window; to be free to go outside and sit or walk, staying as long as was agreeable, was then a small miracle to me, and I used that freedom to get to know my new home. Every day now I would go out into the fields on foot, choosing a direction I hadn't been before and where there were no cattle.

The Butalas owned both the ranch and the hay farm, which, as I have noted, were about forty miles apart. They had bought the hay farm in 1949 because they could not grow enough hay on the ranch itself because the climate was too dry, and relying on purchased hay was risky — there would be years when scarcity made it impossible to buy — and too expensive. The cattle were mostly kept at the ranch, where they wandered the 13,000 acres, grazing and giving birth to their calves and nurturing them. When the worst of winter came, Peter, his family, and fellow ranchers or hired cowboys trailed the herd north and east to the hay farm, where there was shelter in the valley hills and water for them to drink in the river, and where the winter's supply of feed for them was grown, harvested, and stored in bales. When spring came, the herd was trailed back to the ranch. It was such a commonplace annual routine that about the time of the winter move, already the few oldest cows would be waiting patiently at the northeast gate, ready and eager to get to the shelter of the "valley place," which was the hay farm. Thus, we spent part of each year in each place and, once we built the new modern house on the hay farm, often drove back and forth each day. As well, each summer we spent a few weeks in

the valley while Peter did the haying, although the cattle remained
to graze at the ranch.

At the hay farm, sometimes with Sean, I wandered in the hills
to the south across the Frenchman River and to the north climbing
up to the cropped fields that belonged to the neighbours above the
valley, roving through coulees and draws, picking up interesting
small stones and — wonder of wonders — tiny seashells from hills
a hundred feet above where the river now ran. I didn't know land
like this; whatever might be found in it or on it was of great interest to me, and the place seemed full of surprises that I assumed it
was up to me to understand, as if I couldn't belong there if I didn't
comprehend the ground under my feet.

I was initially more interested in the lay of the land, in the
plants, the animals, the birds flying overhead, the schools of fish
I began to spot from a high bank as they made their way down
the river. But soon the subject of dinosaur bones came up, and
by asking questions and turning to books when no one knew the
answers to my questions, I learned that the Eastend area had many
places where the earth had been eroded down through the Ravens-
crag, Cypress Hills, and Wood Mountain formations — that is,
through the Tertiary period right down to the Cretaceous period,
from about 150 million years ago to about 65 million years ago,
when dinosaurs walked the earth. All of us were, in a sense, walking
on dinosaurs. In the Eastend area, where I now lived, no mile-deep
layer of rock and soil, no high-rises, no mountains or tonnes of des-
ert sand or ocean water lay over the dinosaurs; here they were only a
few feet deep, if not right on the surface. Thus, I might conceivably
trip over a fossilized bone, or find a giant tooth or piece of bone
eroded out of the pale, wet clay. It was — extraordinary thought —
more as if here we were walking *among* dinosaurs.

Early one spring as I walked in a particular field, skirting wet
spots and places where patches of snow still lingered, I entered a
wide-mouthed coulee, a place where the high valley wall had been

eroded by rain, snow, and wind to form a winding V heading slightly uphill to the north off the east–west trajectory of the valley. There was little vegetation other than some sage and greasewood, though later in the year stands of prickly pear and pincushion cactus would open their brilliant, delicate, fuchsia or yellow flowers. In my meanderings I came to a place where I noticed an unusual formation that seemed to be sticking out of the earth at the base of the high wall. I went closer and examined it from all directions. Its colour was that dull ochre of the thin, poor soil of the area. It looked to me to be a hip bone of an animal, but one much bigger than a cow or a horse. Much, much bigger. I hardly dared to think it might be a dinosaur bone, but it was hard, rock-like; it hadn't been there before, and I knew that melting snow in the spring and summer rains had been for many years dripping down the wall behind and washing away dirt that would end up on the valley floor. I knew that this was one of the ways in which dinosaurs were revealed.

I nabbed an expert — this took weeks — he came out to see it, examined it, and then, hesitating, maybe saying a silent prayer, he struck it with his light hammer, breaking off a small piece and holding it up as he gazed carefully at it, and finally declared, "What you have here is a concretion." He went on to say that if it had been bone, he would have seen fossilized marrow in the piece he had broken off. But sadly, the inside of the piece looked no different from the outside — all rock, through and through. That was the end of my dream that I had found a dinosaur, but in my disappointment, now more than ever aware of the possibility, I got myself a dinosaur by writing a short story called "The Prize," in which the main character, who is a writer, finds one. (In fact, as far as I can remember, eventually "The Prize" won a prize itself.)

Some years later, on August 16, 1991, when Peter and I had been married for fifteen years, and Sean was — I can't believe it — in his late twenties and married, two paleontologists and the high school principal found the real thing: a T. rex skeleton, or most of one. Such a skeleton had never been found in Saskatchewan before — it was then only the twelfth such found in the world, and at the time, it was the most nearly complete. Because of the shortage of resources in the province to carry out the dig immediately, it was three years before it was announced to the world. So amazing a find was it that people came from as far away as China to take the bus trip out to the quarry and watch it being excavated in the intense summer heat and dryness, in an area that, although well-known to the scientific community, had been previously overlooked not just by Canadians, but by other Saskatchewan people as well.

We all struggled with the truth that the land we stood on every day was the home of dinosaurs, but the unimaginable depth of time between when they had existed and 1994 was just too great for our minds to truly grasp. The paleontologist John Storer tried to explain to people what the world was like in the Cretaceous period by saying, "There was no *there* there then," meaning you couldn't superimpose today's world map onto one of the world then and find anything that matched. The continents 65 million years ago had different shapes; some hadn't yet come into existence, and they were all pretty much somewhere else on the globe from where they are today. When we gazed at the bullet holes in the church at Batoche, a result of the Riel Resistance in 1885, or fingered our dead grandmother's locket on its broken chain, we had a sense of history, but the dinosaurs underfoot defied explanation.

To attempt to deal with the fact of the dinosaurs, most of the community infantilized the creature, who was called Scotty, by marketing it in the form of cute cake pans, on coffee mugs with the picture of a plump, non-reptilian-looking dinosaur on the side, or in the form of cuddly stuffed toys, or candies, where it grinned with childish glee, square-dancing or diving into the swimming pool. Some, perhaps more conscious of what a true wonder the creature actually was, and adhering to Christian fundamentalist beliefs, invented a more manageable provenance for the creature than the one the scientists were proclaiming — that he couldn't be older than 10,000 years, that there was no way to prove that it was 65 million years old. The scientists (nobody said this to me but what other conclusion could you reach?), therefore, must be liars, fools, godless, or all three. Further, they went on to argue, dinosaurs were smaller in the time of Noah's Ark and were able to escape on it, although they died shortly afterward, the food supply having changed, and were fossilized by the weight of the floodwaters. This fairy tale was designed to remove the burden of incomprehensible wonders from the shoulders of its believers; the existence of dinosaurs shattered the myth of the personal, intimate God who speaks every day to the pastor and his friends. I hid my incredulity, knowing these people to be polite, mild, and as decent as the next person.

One of the men working in paleontology who made the find actually said in conversation, much more gratifyingly, that he had been having dreams about "evolution and wonderful things happening." An acquaintance who was a poet and, at the time, the United Church minister gave the matter some serious thought — no doubt he gave a sermon on the subject — and, after pointing out that the dragon is an ancient image in our literature occurring in the Book of Revelation, in *Beowulf*, the first poem extant in English, and in Spenser's *The Faerie Queen*, observed that "the dragon is an image of who we are in the negative sense. It represents the reptilian in us, the dark side we tend to repress. But there's also a nobility, something to respect about it. It's ancient, alien, and dangerous, but it has a power that's beyond us. It threatens our comfortable perspectives and throws us into a kind of chaos." The minister went on to point out that in our struggle to grasp this creature and his or her world, we seem unable to avoid thinking about the T. rex as living among us, and this evokes such dread and terror that we can't cope with it.

Was there another community where everybody was contemplating the great mystery of Creation, not as a myth only, but as a

myth come alive? (The 1912 Piltdown hoax in Britain, to name
one, must have had, briefly, such an effect.) It seemed to me an extraordinary moment in the life of a village far from the great world
capitals, and from the centres of learning: the Sorbonne, Oxford,
Florence, or even those earlier vanished ones such as the ancient
library at Alexandria. The great gap of time between the building
of the pyramids in Egypt (begun in 2560 BC) and the cave paint-
ings at Lascaux, France (at least 20,000 years ago), collapsed into a
more manageable period. But in trying to imagine the time of the
dinosaurs, we faced an impenetrable shroud of nothingness. It was
as if we needed a new way to measure time, a new map of time. This
was, indeed, a kind of chaos, as each of us struggled to integrate this
new-found creature in our midst into his or her map of the world.

From then on, even though I never found even another concretion, never mind an actual dinosaur fossil, I was always conscious
of the unimaginably vast length of time visibly represented in the
mere hay field in which I strolled, hands in my jacket pockets,
thinking. Somehow I had wound up in a place where from the settler's shack I lived in I not only walked by the sunken cellar holes
of missing pioneer houses, the rusted, abandoned implements,
I also walked on the bones of animals that had died 65 million
years ago. In the end, unless you were a scientist, the discovery of
the dinosaur, the reality of it, raised more questions than it could
ever answer.

I had moved from a tight, foreordained world with clear boundaries and rules, governed by procedures, clocks, calendars, and
ringing bells, with daily demands nobody could properly meet and
so had to fudge or fail or obfuscate over, with constant tension
and guilt the result, where simple successes were so rare as to cause

disproportionate exultation. I had gone from that unhappy, tightly wound urban world to one governed by the seasons, by natural forces such as wind, rain, storms, blizzards, and weeks of dry relentless sunshine. In earlier days, the pioneers had planted and harvested and even butchered according to the phases of the moon. In the southwest, you could not ignore the moon and its phases. In so vast a physical space, with measured time retreating into the distance, as I slowly shed my urban, working, single-mother tensions, my brain began to open again. I began to dream the most wonderful dreams, primarily taking place outdoors in some unearthly light and containing the most astounding creatures. These creatures, as I would eventually understand, were insights about the nature of being. Then I remembered my beginnings in the deep forest, with water everywhere, streams, pools, ponds, lakes, rushing wide rivers, and I remembered other visions or dreams. Eventually, parts of my life would begin to link up, to point toward a coherent whole.

I was always striving to know intimately my small world miles from friends and family, to understand the tiniest blossom, the early minute white flower of the moss phlox, the exquisite scent of the gumbo primrose, the way a wild deer gazed at me from across a field or a coyote paused on his meandering trail to nose a flea and consider me as I considered him, the way that I surmised by evidence left behind the unseen paths of the long-dead First Nations people who had camped and worked and prayed and carried out their ceremonies there. They also had lived among the bones of the dinosaurs. I thought initially that if I could know these things thoroughly, some larger, possibly deeper, calamitous understanding of the world would come to me (calamitous because too much for any human to endure). I strained to put all these pieces, these layers of time, together, as if this could be done, as if I could do it, as if it needed doing. I thought there was a place where such purely human responses of wonder, of knowledge of this kind of history, became trivial, fell away entirely if only for a brief period, that brief period being enough time for me to grasp the enormity of the true world.

In my wanderings in the fields belonging to my husband, both at the ranch and at the hay farm, in my intense looking I began to locate items I couldn't quite name. I knew that the stone circles were tipi rings, or so folklore said, and everyone knew, or thought they knew, that the piles of stones were so placed to keep wild animals away from the bones buried beneath, that they were placed over graves, and of course, everybody knew an arrowhead when he or she found one, or a stone hammer. Many were the households, including ours, where a stone hammer was being used as a doorstop, or that had an arrowhead collection (twice I saw Clovis points!) on display as some kind of mark of — what? I'm not sure. Probably that this was a measure of how well you knew your land, of how long you and your father and grandfather had been in the country. It was a kind of boast of your prowess and your authenticity in this place. But most people who displayed their collections and pointed them out to the visitor did so in a mildly puzzled way, as if by finding and collecting these artifacts they had still not managed to join themselves with them. These relics of the past were still, in some indefinable sense, a mystery. Long after Peter was gone, I visited a modern house out on the land that had on its front lawn two actual iron-bound wooden barrels full of such artifacts as I've listed, all washed and polished and sitting there, serving no purpose whatsoever.

I think that digging out the past and preserving it is not merely an avocation for a few, whimsical and time-filling, but an authentic drive to know who we are. It also represents an authentic drive to honour and respect in particular the people who, whether they knew it or not, or meant to do it or not, contributed in some degree — small or great — to who we are today. Thus, when I hear of farmers or ranchers refusing to allow archaeologists on their land, who remove ancient stone features such as cairns and tipi rings in order to use the stones for other purposes, or in order to plow the land under the features, I am always angered. Even the fact of the precious Clovis points sitting in private houses when they should be in museum collections where all of us can see them seems to me selfish (not to mention illegal). Memory plays an enormous part in our ability to function each day, even to get dressed in the morning — think of a person with advanced dementia or Alzheimer's disease who without memory is no longer the individual we knew and loved — but it also is a collective power. It magnifies us, gives us meaning in the scheme of things. This was, in part, what drove me to study the past of the southwest.

One day during my first year as a resident it finally crystallized that I hadn't seen any Indigenous people around on the streets or in the stores, and that none lived in the village or on the land surrounding it. In Saskatchewan, Aboriginal people were a part of daily life, even if there was a hard although unspoken boundary between us and them. In the bush where I was born they had sometimes worked for my father in the sawmill and pitched their tipis in the field behind our log house, where the women's lives sometimes — rarely — crossed with ours; after that, in villages, they would come through in the summer, mostly in horse-drawn wagons, and the women would sell wild berries they had picked or rag rugs they had made. In Saskatoon, it was probably not until the sixties that they became a familiar part of city life, and in the years that followed, they began to be lawyers, doctors, teachers, social workers, and full-time artists and, occasionally, legislators and politicians.

In a province where, according to the 2011 census, 10 percent of the population was First Nations (having grown from a lower number, perhaps 6 to 7 percent) and in which 11.3 percent of the total Canadian population of Aboriginal people (1.4 million) lived, to suddenly find myself in an area where there was almost never a single Aboriginal person anywhere I went seemed ominous. When I asked, I was told that they could be found in Maple Creek, to the north on the far side of the Cypress Hills, and then, that they had a small reserve up in the hills, which did not answer my question as to why they weren't a part of our daily lives as they were in the places in the province from where I had come.

In my 2005 non-fiction book, *Lilac Moon: Dreaming of the Real West*, I wrote about the long, sorrowful, and savage story of what we Euro-Canadians did to the First Peoples of this land, a story that ought by law to be taught in all schools. Earlier, in doing research for *The Perfection of the Morning*, I had located and drawn on a shocking article by Western historian John Tobias (1942–2009) of Red Deer College in Red Deer, Alberta, called "Canada's Subjugation of the Plains Cree, 1879–1885" (first published in *Canadian Historical Review* in 1983). It tells the painful story of how the government of Canada rid itself of the Plains Cree, or did its best to do so, by starving them into submission. This deliberate government policy was carried out by the North-West Mounted Police, now the Royal Canadian Mounted Police (RCMP).

The plains peoples were weakened by the demise of the bison, but for thousands of years, until the contact era, the number of people was small enough and the habitual round of hunting such that the numbers of bison grew, rather than decreased. Once contact was established and the bison hide became valuable to whites as well as to Indigenous people, hunting was stepped up, until those millions of bison shrank to a handful. From the late 1870s up to about 1885, people began to starve, and searched in vain for herds, and when they were desperate enough, they turned to the usurpers of their lands for food, to be told they would be given rations only if they "took treaty." Most of them did so, and any chiefs who held out, in their wisdom knowing well what lay ahead, were so pressured by their hungry band members that eventually they acquiesced. "Taking treaty" meant that (although this was negotiated doggedly by the Native leaders) they would leave southwest Saskatchewan and the Cypress Hills area, where at the height of the crisis thousands had congregated, and go to reserves to the north or to the east. According to historian Blair Stonechild, "Between 1880 and 1885 the Indian population dropped from 32,549 to 20,170." As I have noted, only a small group of stubborn people refused to leave, led by a Cree man named Nekaneet. They survived in the Cypress Hills, where eventually they were given a reserve called Nekaneet. The First Nations leaders, not being fools, had done their best to be granted contiguous reserves, which would have meant that almost all of southwest Saskatchewan would have been one vast Indian land, but this the authorities would never allow. That explains why in 1975 or 1976 one could travel through southwest Saskatchewan, aside from Maple Creek, without seeing an Indigenous face. And yet, as terrible as this story is, that is also how I was able to find scrapers and flakes, circles and cairns everywhere on unplowed land. If I was starting to understand that we were walking on dinosaurs, I was also starting to comprehend that we were all living on First Nations land.

One day Peter told me to draw my eye along the top line of the hills until I came to the place where the valley wall turned north, and there, at the very top of that point, was a bump. Eventually we went to see what the "bump" actually was. It was an Indigenous cairn, a large one, in the highest corner of a farmer's field, with a long view out over the valley in three directions. We did not know ourselves what the cairn represented, but we did know that one just like it on the same side of the valley, but twenty or more miles away, had been excavated by a couple of kids, I think in the thirties, and that eventually archaeologists had come and done a proper job and had found the arranged bones of five individuals beneath it that they dated to about twenty-five hundred years ago. We thus could assume that this cairn was actually a grave.

These strange hillsides dotted with rocks of all kinds and sizes — not really hills for the most part, but the sloping valley walls — had once been covered with as much as a two-mile-thick coating of glacial ice. The melting back of glaciers in this area had

begun as long as ten to fourteen thousand years ago. Thus, the artifacts and features couldn't be any older than when the land was
first bared after the retreat of the glaciers. As everybody knows,
glaciers scrape and gouge in one place while dropping deposits in
another, and they carry material from one place and may well drop
it a thousand miles or more away. The field I walked in contained a
surprising, almost amusing mixture of all kinds of rocks side by side
or on top of each other and from sometimes faraway places, resting
beside rocks formed on the very place they sat. I remembered: igne-
ous, metamorphic, sedimentary. I knew granite when I saw it (or I
thought I did), and many of the rocks in the field looked as if they
were made of compressed mud or earth; I was sure they had to be
sedimentary. I bought an elementary-level book on rocks, but once
I had mastered the most rudimentary information, I gave up, never
having developed a deep interest in the subject.

A lot more interesting to me were the tracks, trails, and evidence of Indigenous life in the field. If I could not fully grasp
the distance between my current self and the dinosaurs, and found
rocks themselves barely interesting, it was much more within my
comprehension to accept the lives of Indigenous peoples, on the
land around us.

I walked the field, year after year, for thirty years. I even wrote
a book, *Wild Stone Heart: An Apprentice in the Fields*, about it. I
began learning things about the more recent past, the past since
the retreat of the glaciers. I bolstered what I saw with my own eyes
by a search for books that would answer questions such as one of
my first pressing queries: *Who were the people who left these traces of
their civilization behind?* And *Why are there no First Nations people
in the area where I live when it is covered with the features and artifacts of their ancestors?* Toward the last of my years on the land, I
was appointed to the arm's-length board that manages money the
provincial government provides to support professional people as
well as civic-minded amateur committees working in the heritage

area. Not only did I learn a multitude of things about my province both pre- and post-contact, but I began to be acquainted with archaeologists, some of them specializing in the area where I lived.

Whether they meant to or not, they began to teach me. They pointed me to books I might read, or even sent me fascinating papers they had written: I remember in particular David Meyer's *The Red Earth Crees, 1860–1960*, which concerns the Indigenous people in the area where I was born and spent my early childhood. One of the archaeologists, Margaret Hanna, after visiting with an elder and a First Nations man who acted as liaison in such matters between First Nations interests and (I presume) government and private interests, would later bring a crew who set to work photographing and mapping one of the most fascinating features in the field.

Besides the most obvious features, which were the cairns and the stone circles we thought might be tipi rings, there were rocks from which it was clear chunks had been broken off to make tools. The flakes lay scattered below them. As well, there was a possible bison drive line, and a circle not more than a foot in diameter at another high point with a flat stone buried in its centre. Other clearly man-made features, including the largest circle that on examination I, at least, believed to be a turtle effigy, were harder to name. This was the one mapped one hot summer afternoon by Dr. Hanna's crew. I owe the archaeologists a debt too large to ever be repaid.

One day I thought that it would be possibly informative to pretend that I was a First Nations woman from pre-contact times and that the season was not winter, and that we were not at war. What if I came into this field planning to stay a few days? Suppose I entered from the east? I went to the east edge of the field, considered, and decided that I would not walk at the top of the field, where my silhouette could be seen from a long distance; that, travelling on foot and quite likely with a child on my back, I wouldn't be climbing each hill but would negotiate the easiest path — that is, the middling-height draws between the hills. I set out, picking

my way carefully, and at the first draw — I could hardly believe
it — I saw a couple of small tipi rings, off to one side of the invisible path I'd chosen. They were the size my reading had told me
"the People" used when they were travelling. This was a past that
I could grasp, and I felt in some way that I had connected to the
people of the past.

After I had begun to try to see patterns in the things I was finding and where I was finding them, I understood that the women,
who were the ones who prepared the hides and also the foods and
the sage and sweetgrass for ceremonies, liked to sit on these low hills
to work. This was where I found scrapers. I knew very soon that to
pick these artifacts up and take them home was not only against the
law but pointless. Out of their milieu they lost their story, became
more and more meaningless. Sometimes I even wondered if, when I
took them home, I was committing a crime against those ancestors
who had passed through, lived for brief periods, fought and died
there and whose remains were buried all around me. So I left them
where they were.

My research told me the complex story of people who had
crossed this country and camped in it long before there were any
national or international boundaries on the continent, had stayed
to hunt and fish and gather the edible plants with which they were
so familiar. First Nations groups each had, of course, their own
territory and their own agreements about who could go in safety
on the other's land and under what circumstances. External factors
post-contact were very important. Smallpox epidemics were devas-
tating to a people who lived far from the crowded, unsanitary cities of Europe and North America. One had so weakened the Gros
Ventre and the Shoshone as to drive them farther south into the
United States. But the major factor was the slaughter of the bison.
It is reported that the last bison was seen in the Cypress Hills area in
the late 1870s, but prior to that, the bulk of the remaining animals
had escaped farther and farther west out of Cree territory and into

Blackfoot lands. When the Cree had run out of them in their own lands for food (and the dozens of other purposes for which they were used), they began to make dangerous forays farther west into Blackfoot territory.

Not long after I had read about this historical period, my sister brought her coastal First Nations friend, an elder and fluent speaker of her own language, with her to visit. Never one to miss an opportunity to find out anything I could about the field, I told the woman about it, and we made a foray through it where nothing much was said. That evening the three of us walked down the dirt trail that follows the river between the house yard, the hay fields, and the hills beyond. We talked about nothing much as we strolled, and darkness began to fall, and then, suddenly she turned, went into the hay field, and scrambled up to the top of a big round bale, a feat in itself, but she did it as if it had stairs attached to its side.

She called out to the field in her own language. A moment later she called to us, asking couldn't we see *the people* moving fast about the field, which we could not, but both my sister and I heard the eerie, wailing call that came back to us from deep, deep in the darkness of the hillside. Later, we came to believe that the cairns must be graves. The field was more or less along the boundary between the Blackfoot and Cree territories, and we knew from historical accounts that as food dried up in Cree territory, the Cree moved west to encroach on the Blackfoot territory, and battles were fought. These battles culminated in a famous one in 1870 at the junction of the Oldman River and the St. Mary River in what is now near Lethbridge, Alberta, where many were killed, especially Cree, who lost more than two hundred warriors. After that, the Blackfoot and the Cree reached an accord that allowed all to hunt for food on Blackfoot land. I hasten to point out that this is the historians' account of what happened. I do not know the Cree stories, nor the Blackfoot version of events.

And yet, one suspects an uneasy truce. Recently when a distant

relative of mine by marriage, whose father is Cree, married a Blackfoot man and reported, laughing, that all the Blackfoot women who
met her declared at once, cheerfully, to her husband-to-be, "Oh! You
are marrying a Cree woman!" I could imagine their eyes — those of
the husband-to-be and the women of his reserve — meeting, and
in their gazes the knowledge of the old history of alliances and wars,
of acrimony and death, and, finally, truce. I envision a day when
our schools begin teaching history that includes what is known of
the movements and belief systems of the Indigenous people of this
country, accepting this as real history, and as vital as that of the
nations and continents from which the settlers came.

The elder who came to the field said softly to us, gazing up to
the cairns on a nearby hill, "Lot of people died here." And another
First Nations woman I met said she knew all the stories about where
I lived and would come and tell them to me, but she never did, and
I was not able to find her again. I accepted ruefully that it had been
decided that I was not to know. Yet, with our continuing history
of appalling racism toward the Indigenous peoples, I cannot blame
her (or others) for this. Slowly, over the years, I came to know by
these ways recounted above that the field was not just stones and
hardpan, wide patches of creeping juniper, greasewood, sage, and
cactus: the field was a repository of Canadian history.

I had learned about the cairns and what they probably represented;
I had found scrapers and flakes and rocks where I could see the
stone had been broken off to make points and other tools. One day
I even found a cylindrical stick about six inches long with a diameter of about an inch (or more), carved out of white quartz, and a
small white sphere beside it of the same material. As had become
my practice, I left them there on the hillside. When I went back to

find them again, I could not, even though I had marked mentally with great care where they were. I did eventually find both a white quartz stick and sphere, but they had been so damaged by age and the elements that I wasn't sure they were the ones I saw the first time. This is just a mystery and it has no explanation. An archaeologist friend suggested that the stick and the sphere might have been used for gaming or in spiritual practices.

There was another layer to the field that I have touched upon in this chapter, and that is the layer where Spirit ruled, where the world of Spirit opened to allow a faithful, respectful observer in. It existed, whatever it was, for me as did the stone cairns and the rings of stones we identified as tipi rings, which some undoubtedly were.

One of these odd circles was on the top of a long, flat hill that ran east–west, at the outer edge of the field and well above the flatland, but far below the highest point. This was a large circle, much larger than the average tipi ring, and it had, at four points around it (or maybe there were five, I've forgotten), small gatherings of stones that might once have been outlines of circles attached to it. (In time I would realize, or come to believe, that the structure was, or had been, a depiction of a turtle, a symbol of great power and meaning in the First Nations world.) It took me a very long time to see this last, but on the short westerly end of the hill, there was a pathway marked out in stones that led to the circle above.

Once, when I knew a good deal more about the practices of the ancient peoples, on a summer solstice evening, a time I knew by then to be of utmost importance to the plains people, a cloudless evening when the light was as pure as I've seen it in my life so that one might feel it was palpable and filled with force, I dared to climb up into the field and to go to the base of this hill with the path leading up it to the circle on top. The sun threw glowing red light from along the western horizon behind me, across the fields to where I stood at the bottom of the hill. I was beginning to understand. I thought this was a religious site, that at the appropriate moment the sun's rays would strike perfectly up the path toward the hill, and so I waited, moments only. The sun's rays at the moment of the sun's setting didn't quite match the trajectory of the path running up the hillside, and I would learn that over the centuries those rays would have altered slightly in their direction so that one might reasonably think that maybe several hundred or more years earlier, the path had been marked so that the rays went straight up it. Up I went, slowly, with much trepidation, aware I was never alone in that place, no matter that no flesh-and-blood humans accompanied me, and when I got to the top at the place where the path ended, I stopped dead in my tracks.

Before me, a vertical wall — it has always seemed to me a translucent wall, although perhaps *veil* is a better word — of red light was thrown up between me and the stone circle I had come to see on the other side of it. I was disoriented, thought I must have made a mistake, wondered for a second if I was on the wrong hill. In my astonishment, I thought to look along the ground in front of me from where the red wall of light seemed to emanate and saw something that in all my trips there I had never before noticed. There was a rough line of rocks that ran north to south, half-buried by time and the blowing, dirt-filled winds, by earth and sparse grass, and that partially misaligned and misshapen line seemed indeed to be so designed that the most powerful red light coming from the sun behind it just before it sank below the horizon on the summer solstice struck it, and threw up the wall of glowing orange-red light.

I didn't tell the story this way in *Wild Stone Heart*: I was afraid then to tell too much for fear that people would just write me off as an unhinged person, so I left out that wall of red light. But since I wrote that book more than fifteen years ago, I have grown braver. On that evening so many years ago I stepped through the veil of light and into the middle of the circle, where I stood in silence for only a few seconds until the light began to die, and darkness was filling the hollows and creeping up the hillsides. Then I stepped out of the circle and ran across the hay fields to where Peter was running a tractor.

He stopped for me, I climbed up the tractor's narrow ladder, he leaning over to grasp my hand to pull me up the last step, and I leaned against him, grateful for his warmth and solidity as he drove us back into the yard. I didn't tell him what I'd seen; he didn't know that I was in awe, my awe tempered by fear and a powerful sense that I — we — lived in the heart of mystery, surrounded by the past of people we did not know, but who seemed to know us.

There is one more layer of history present and visible to a careful observer on that one hundred acres I have been referring to as "the field." It also has what was surely a cellar depression, and other signs that somebody once tried to homestead, if not in that field where he built his house, then just below it on the valley bottom. Whoever he was, he couldn't have survived more than a year there. The presence of that cellar depression is another reminder of the next layer of civilization to occupy the land of the southwest: the settlers.

In 1872 the government of Canada passed the Dominion Lands Act, whose purpose was to populate the prairie provinces by opening them for farming. This was also deemed necessary in order to secure the prairies from the American conviction called "manifest destiny," which held that settlers were destined to claim their territory and establish institutions far and wide across the North American continent. If the land was already occupied by Canadians, the American desire to fill it would be stymied. Part of the national policy of the period was the building of a cross-country railway. This was completed in 1885, but further branch lines had to be built in order to reach into all the newly settled areas and to help settlers transport themselves and their goods. Any village not close enough to a railway branch line soon faded and died.

Under the act, for a fee of $10, and by fulfilling certain other conditions such as breaking so much land per year, building a dwelling on it, and remaining in residence for a minimum of six months of the year, any adult male could acquire 160 acres, with a provision to acquire another 160, called a pre-emption, roughly when the conditions on the first 160 acres were met. At first settlement was slow, but when Prime Minister Sir Wilfrid Laurier appointed Clifford Sifton in 1896 as the federal minster of the interior, Sifton began to vigorously promote the settlement of Western Canada in the United States, Britain, and especially in east-central Europe. Unfortunately, the agents spreading out through Europe exaggerated (or simply didn't tell the truth about) conditions, insisting that "the rain follows the plow" (patently untrue), and that the weather on the prairies was balmy all year round and the soil miraculously fertile (these last two, for the most part, worse than not true). In some places the soil was indeed abundantly fertile, but in others it certainly was not, and as for the insistence on balmy weather — well, one forty-below winter day would clear up any misapprehensions on that score.

Over the next twenty-five or so years a quarter of a million settlers came from the United States alone, and in total over two million from Europe, Britain, the United States, as well as Ontario and Quebec, and mostly under difficult conditions and suffering considerable hardship, they began to create farms out of the native prairie and into the parklands. Everywhere small towns and villages sprang up to support them, and with the railway crawling past (some but not all of) their towns, the prairie provinces went in a few years from being "empty" (rarely were the Indigenous people counted in such a declaration) to being occupied and "civilized." The Dominion Lands Act was closed in 1930, but by then, just about all the free land of the prairie West was taken.

Government preparations to receive this flood of people from Europe and the British Isles were inadequate. People were allowed to come in the late summer or in the fall when no gardens could be planted and no food supply was otherwise available for them. Most of these people had no money to speak of except for the basic amount needed to pay the $10 fee to secure their homestead land, and to buy farming implements and an animal or two, no "fall-back" position such as staying in the city until spring and then going out to find their land. Many of them did not speak English; many were from towns and cities and had never farmed. That any-body survived at all in those days is a wonder.

It was hard for everyone, the men who never stopped work-ing, the children who were expected to work every minute they weren't in school or asleep, but it was especially hard on the women. Peter's mother, Alice Graham Butala, a highly intelligent woman who had been raised in a longer-established farming community in southern Manitoba (the Graham farm there was established in 1885), often said that the rules that applied to the original settlers in order for them to maintain ownership of their 160 acres made no sense. She was referring chiefly to the strict residency requirements which meant that, with the pre-emption (another 160 acres), all farm families were isolated. But, as she would point out, it was the women who were particularly isolated. They rarely went "to town," unlike the men, who travelled there over rough roads to get parts for their machinery, or to have things fixed, or to pick up the mail, or to buy feed. She would know about this, having married her husband in the early thirties and lived with him and their growing family on the ranch that is still remote today, into the mid-sixties. When Peter's father, George, became ill, Peter had to take him out to the hospital on his snowmobile to the truck that in winter he kept four miles south in the village of Divide, where the road was maintained in winter.

She told me that year after year of prolonged isolation caused an immense loneliness, a yearning just to see the face of another woman; no family could fully satisfy such deep-seated human needs. As well, the roads were poor to non-existent in the early years, which made for serious difficulty in delivering the services settlers needed: medical care, schooling for the children, supplies, and building materials. She declared that it would have been more reasonable if small villages were established, with the farm owner-workers driving out each day to the land to work as is done in Europe, the very Europe from which Peter's father had fled.

I think of my mother, married in 1935, going into the bush to live around 1937. Eventually she had her own mother living a mile to the north, for a while, and two miles to the south, one of her sisters. But when she woke in the night (on two occasions) having a miscarriage, when our father was away and she had only toddlers at home, there was no one to run up or down the grassy trail through the forest in the night to either of her female relatives for help. To the day she died she was proud of how she handled the bleeding, which fortunately eventually stopped on its own, and always said with pride that, both times, in the morning she stuffed the sheet she had wrapped around herself, now blood-soaked, into the burning barrel and burned it. "And no one even knew." Multiply that story by a thousand-fold, or perhaps even more.

If the promised prosperity really had come in the first few years, all of this would have been bearable, but it did not come. The homesteading failure rate was about 60 percent in the worst areas (overall it is estimated to be about 50 percent; in Saskatchewan it was set at about 57 percent), and to some extent it had been predicted long before the land was opened for settlers. For the Butalas had settled in the Palliser Triangle, an area of land of about 73,000 square miles of the Great Plains of North America, extending through southern Saskatchewan and into Alberta with its apex south of Edmonton, although if you look at early maps which vary somewhat, and read the first description of it, you would find that southwestern Manitoba was originally included. For the most part, the soil in the triangle is poor and light brown in colour, and is known for its aridity. When I lived there, the average annual precipitation was surprisingly only about twelve inches. Yet the climate is extreme.

The triangle takes its name from John Palliser, an Irishman sent by the British on expeditions between 1857 and 1860 — he was preceded by the Henry Youle Hind expedition — to evaluate the suitability of these western lands for farming. Palliser declared them to be mostly unfit for it because of the too-arid climate, the poor quality of the soil, and the lack of trees for fuel and building. This too had been the conclusion of the Hind report. A further expedition in 1872 by botanist John Macoun, a report that was most optimistic and enthusiastic (as apparently was the man himself), turned the tables by declaring most of the area to be fertile and good for farming, encouraging the federal government, which was looking for just such an excuse, to open this area to settlers. It is said that Macoun must have made his expedition during an unusually wet year so that the country was flourishing, instead of in its more usual state of near desert-like conditions. Whatever the reasons, it suited the government to populate an area so close to the American border with loyal new Canadians.

When I was only eighteen in 1958, I had a part-time job in the archives then at the University of Saskatchewan, where my work was to take the stacks of files of the original settlers and gather a certain few pertinent facts — land description, names of settlers, years of ownership, correspondence with the government — and reduce it to a single filing card. Every once in a while I would come across a handwritten letter, sometimes composed by a neighbour because the settler in question was illiterate in English, telling the most indelibly sad story of why the land hadn't been "proved up" yet, according to the requirements of the Dominion Lands Act. Such stories: *Over the winter my wife and all my children died of*

diphtheria. . . . I walked a hundred miles to [the nearest small town]
to look for work and when I didn't find any, I walked all the way back
again. . . . A neighbour brought us food when we had only frozen po-
tatoes to eat, and saved our lives. . . . My wife died in childbirth. . . .
These were not nicely typed missives on thick vellum; they were
written more often on scraps of paper, scrawled, often with errors
in grammar and syntax. But they brought home to me in a way the
government documents or the history books I was reading in class
could never capture the reality of the despair and pain of far too
many of those people. That I remember them so well nearly sixty
years after I saw them is evidence of that.

Where did the women out on the land find nourishment for
their female souls other than in their children, and indeed, how
could they hope to raise truly educated children in such an environment? It isn't just the simple loneliness, as it is the sense of bleakness
of the life for those who couldn't fully hide from themselves the
need for "something more" that their hearts yearned for, the utter
lack of opportunities beyond marriage and children that slowly kills
the female soul. And if you happened to come from a non-English-
speaking country, how complete the alienation must have been.

This is not the story the people of the area tell you, or, if they
do, they tell it to you in dribs and drabs in an almost mythic way:
a single tale of a young man going white-haired overnight after he
had lost another crop; of the row of babies' graves in the cemetery
who died by fire (a constant worry in frame buildings) or disease;
of the boy riding his horse every day in all weather, miles to school,
and one day dragged to death by it; of the relative losing his way in
a blizzard and found frozen in a field or on the trail; of the women
rendered mad or nearly so by overwork, too many pregnancies and
children, and unending loneliness. The primary story is the one of
how hard the early settlers worked so that their descendants, today's
owners, might rest in the prosperity they claim today. But such a
bitter beginning extracts a toll from the generations that follow.

People don't emerge optimistic from such a history; they are more likely to be proud, careful with their money, suspicious of outsiders. Kindness can be thin and rare. Generosity is too often seen as foolishness. That original promise of free land, of salvation, hangs there in the air still.

Of course, such inherited hardship also creates kind people. The all-night schoolhouse dances in the early days, the fowl suppers, the neighbourliness, the love among family members, the devotion of mothers and fathers, the respect of young women for old and of middle-aged men for the old men who gave their lives to their small enterprises.

I was starting to understand that from the extinction of the dinosaurs to the heart-rending history of the First Nations people and then of so many people who left Europe filled with hope for the future and who met only with failure and loss, hardship and suffering, the history of this land was in many ways a tragic one.

Peter, being human (and judged by me), had his shortcomings, but he knew one thing with every fibre of his being: how precious his land was. He knew too, though, that he was very fortunate in that he could afford to keep his grass in excellent condition because he hadn't married — deliberately, he claimed — until he was forty-one and established financially. He told me many times that by marrying young, men guaranteed that the financial pressure involved in raising a family meant that they would not be able to take any of their land out of production in order to rest it for a year or several years as he sometimes did; that they would have to put too many head of cattle on their grass, which would result in damage to the grass, and as the roots weakened, invader plants such as crested wheatgrass, or forbs such as sage, would crowd out the nutritious and cattle-friendly native plants. As our years together passed, he cut back his herd more and more in order to preserve the quality of the prairie under his control.

I admired a good deal more about him than only his love and care of his land. He minded his own business, kept silent when others might have gossiped or spread cruel stories. He placed a high value on his father's dictum that he should care for his mother and his sisters and tried his best to look out for them, and did his — admittedly, distant — best where Sean was concerned, wanting to take responsibility, yet careful not to overstep boundaries for a boy who was close to his father. He loved his old friends and was loyal to them too, the men he had cowboyed with when he was young, and whose rodeo adventures he followed and admired. He had struggled too hard to maintain what he had acquired to be wildly generous (despite what some of the neighbours apparently thought, he was never a rich man), but he helped a number of people, quietly, behind the scenes. He didn't seem to have any ambition to become a prominent community member other than by being a successful, knowledgeable rancher, one who could be turned to for advice about cattle or horses; if asked, he willingly gave it.

The older he got, the more he cared for his animals and the harder it became for him to do some of the things that the ranching enterprise required. Castrating young bulls or horses was something he would have preferred never to do again, and he particularly loathed de-horning as very painful to the animal and needlessly cruel; he even commented with disgust on the large size of some brands on animals we saw in the sale ring or elsewhere as causing them unnecessary pain. He refused to try to produce bigger and bigger calves at birth because of the danger and suffering this caused his cows. For most of the years we were married and sold cattle, we didn't plan for early calves in order to sell them in the same fall, but sold instead "big" steers, those a year or even two years old. Thus, having very large calves at birth wasn't necessary as, by the time the animals were sold, they had had plenty of time to grow to a good size. If this attitude to ranching sounds unusual, I suspect that it is, but more than once coming home from helping work animals on another ranch he remarked that some of the older men agreed with him. Once he came home saying he would never help out on that ranch again because the family who owned it did not look after its animals well enough, didn't keep them in clean bedding or get them the help of the veterinarian in time, especially did not recognize their right to be free of pain. Being "hard" on your animals is a quality in a rancher or farmer that is detested by rural people of quality, of which Peter was one.

All of these were things that I loved about him, was sometimes in awe over, because, taken together, in my experience they were rare. And of course, they culminated in his ultimate determination that his land would not be sold to farmers and broken into separate pieces when he died; that the land he so cherished and nurtured, gave even his potential prosperity to, would be kept in one block and never broken; that the native prairie would be kept, in perpetuity, in excellent condition. He dreamt, too, of the day when there would be native bison back living on it again. I was thirty-six when I married Peter, and it took me time to appreciate the quiet depth of his character. Though both of us might be embarrassed by declarations of undying love (I am sure he is looking over my shoulder as I write this, and can imagine his sheepish grin and his turning away if I had written anything like that), I never stopped thinking myself fortunate to have him as my husband.

Nobelist writer J. M. Coetzee remarked that every writer's life in art goes through three stages and "in the first you find, or pose for yourself, a great question." In my early days in Saskatchewan, living on layers of history, this was my "great question": *What is a human life worth?*

Of course, I'm not sure I knew that at the time, formulating it explicitly only in hindsight. The more I found out about prairie history and the history of the region where I'd gone to live with Peter, and also remembering my own family history, the more I pondered that question. One of the first and strongest of many things that struck me about the local culture was, delivered without fanfare or even the raising of a voice, the wisdom that came from the mouths of people with little or no formal education. Usually from old people, and I marvelled at how much suffering they must have seen, and how much thinking they must have done about it, and how humbly accepting of it they seemed to be. Coming from a university community as I had, I had grown to expect that you had to have at least a PhD and have written many books, and read many more, to be able to speak wisdom, and I was humbly disabused of such a notion.

Of the number of things I wanted to do in my books, one of the more important ones was to convey to the dubious urban reader the wisdom of rural people, this in order to show that to dismiss them out of hand, as was the habit of most urban people, was absolute foolishness. I wanted very much to show in my books that there are other ways to gain wisdom and understanding of the human condition than in the study of the writings of others, and that a rural life, seen as ignominious at the least, was worth every bit as much as an urban life lived in sophisticated surroundings, and with many more opportunities of the kind rural people could usually only dream of: wide travel, meetings with the famous and esteemed of the world, and familiarity with great discoveries and great music, with literature and the visual arts. I marvelled over how a life lived so close to the bone could teach so much about the human soul.

When I thought about this matter, I would lift my eyes and gaze out across the acres of grass empty of people and buildings

all the way to the distant horizon, feeling the wind playing around
me, it rarely stopping unless at sunset or at sunrise, when the world
seemed to be catching its breath to pause in wonder, as I was, gazing
at the luminescence of land and sky. Living in the bosom of nature
all their lives, I thought, how could rural people not be fully aware,
even in their blood and bones, of the mystery of human existence?
This was what I ached to write, although I did not know how to do
it, and could only keep trying and trying again, and knowing with
each publication that I had failed in my aim, had fallen short of it. I
often thought of the old saw that says that every writer has only one
book in him or her and just keeps writing it over and over again.
That was me, I thought, and book after book, I dreamt of the day
when I would finally get it right, knowing all the while that without
Peter to guide and teach me, I couldn't do it.

5

Home on the Range

By the time I came to live with him, Peter was alternating between living on the ranch and on the hay farm. He was at the hay farm not only when the cattle were there, but also in the spring and summer, as I've said, to irrigate (a twenty-four-hour-a-day job for two weeks usually twice each summer), and he had to be there for the weeks it took to hay. This seasonal migration Peter and I continued to do, moving back and forth between the hay farm with its log house built in 1912 and the ranch with its simple settler's house. During the third year of our marriage, we built a much-needed house, a simple three-bedroom bungalow that looked to us like a palace after living in bathroom-less, central-heating-less, mouse-riddled homes for such a long time. We built it at the hay farm because Peter wouldn't hear of building it at the ranch, saying that in the worst months of the winter the wind never stopped blowing there, that the roads were mostly closed — he had once been stuck there in winter for six full weeks all by himself — and that it was generally just too uncomfortable for cattle, horses, or, given the living accommodations, humans.

The two of us already had experience in living in the most primitive of conditions: I in a log house in Saskatchewan's then nearly trackless bush country without electricity, telephones, running water, or bathrooms, and he at the ranch on the northern Great Plains of North America in a four-room, jerry-built house not much better than a cabin. But my family had moved on, bit by bit, to regular houses in an urban environment — Sean had lived only in modern dwellings — and Peter's family members eventually left for better ways of living, too, but until I came along, Peter had continued into his early forties in these same minimalist buildings.

We were not the first to finally build a decent house. In those early years, I recall, one of the favourite subjects of conversation among the women was the need for a new house, or who was finally getting a new house. The women complained mostly of what I too found the hardest to deal with: the mice that could not be stopped no matter how many traps were set or holes plugged. We had an atavistic reaction to the very sound of them scratching in the walls. The cold floors, too cold for babies and toddlers to play on, and the cold wind and dust sweeping in through leaky window frames and sashes were the other chief complaints. Space was very limited in those houses, too, and we would often comment on how, in the early days, large numbers of people had somehow managed to live in the tiniest of houses that, in addition to the lack of space, hadn't a single closet or storage space. That, we would tell each other, was because nobody owned anything more than a change or two of clothing.

Peter's mother (who died in 1984, seven years after our marriage) recalled that during the Great Depression, with its accompanying

ten-or-so-year drought and crop failures, many people in the southwest were reduced to living in conditions not much better than in
third-world countries. The bottom was reached when, in a treeless
land, settlers were reduced to burning cow pies, or "chips," for fuel
to keep warm and with which to cook. She spoke the truth, although she was less than popular for saying it. Peter once told me
how much he admired his mother for her plain speaking, how lie
or prevarication was beyond her, no matter what such truth-telling
cost her. I used to wonder sometimes, as many women do, if that
was why he was attracted to me, perhaps flattering myself in the
process.

About the time that Peter began to build a better house, a lot of
other families did the same, and before too many years had passed,
everyone began to be more surprised at the people who didn't have
a new house than at those who did. These new places were almost
always the commonplace three-bedroom aluminum- or vinyl-sided
white bungalows of Western Canada, but a few people built what
seemed to the rest of us to be mansions — very large frame houses
with fancy windows and actual driveways and attached garages.
They were usually the people with more land, or better land, or
ones who also had a tidy income from rent for the oil wells located
on their land. Twenty oil wells alone could at that time add up to a
year's income in themselves, never mind the income from the sale
of crops or cattle. But so many oil wells on a farm or ranch was the
exception rather than the rule. As for the sale of crops, the local
farmer was almost always beholden to the international market,
which had since the Great Depression or earlier been handled by
the provincial wheat pools, and by the Canadian Wheat Board (a
process referred to as single-desk selling), so that farmers, who in
those days often didn't have a high level of formal education, did
not have to face these mysteries themselves, and so that Western
farmers together had some clout in the increasingly competitive
marketplace.

I was happy in our new house. It wasn't elaborate, but it was comfortable. After it became our headquarters, we continued to travel back and forth whenever the work required it, or we moved into the small frame ranch house where Peter had spent his life for a couple of weeks while he (and usually I too) rode the cattle checking for accidents or illness or broken fences and escapees that had to be brought back. In the fall he got in the crops, or hayed the few sloughs in years when there was enough moisture to produce wild hay. Dugouts were dug, fencing was repaired (a job that never ended). When the cattle were at the ranch from spring into late fall, we would stay there for long periods. For a dozen years we were constantly back and forth the forty miles between the two places, and often, when I wasn't needed, and after I had begun writing on one of the first personal computers that were too bulky and inconvenient to move, I would pack him a lunch rather than going with him merely to cook a meal or two. He began to come back at night, too, if he possibly could. He was aging, and he liked a warm house and a comfortable bed over the sparse, uncomfortable bachelor arrangements at the ranch as much as I did. Like most men, he wanted a real home of his own.

We were becoming hybrids, the two of us: one foot in the past and the wild prairie, and the other foot in the present of wireless technology, jet planes available for distant holidays, space exploration and central heating. Like so many rural people of his generation, Peter was conflicted, on the one hand marvelling at the past and his homesteader and rancher heroes, wanting in a way to go back to it, chasing wild horses on horseback with his father, living the free and easy life of the cowboy with other cowboys (but as the only son of a rancher, unable to be footloose as a real cowboy was). On the other hand, he became a pilot of small planes as well as a lover of all the new gadgetry, reading agricultural newspapers by the dozens in order to learn about the latest discoveries and inventions, yearning to get on a jet and fly all over the world. Yet he did not yearn to be someone else: a banker, an economist, a geologist, or a crop scientist. For the most part, he loved his life. And he loved his land.

In *The Perfection of the Morning* I told a story about how, in the first year of our marriage, on a hot summer afternoon when Peter had gone out to ride through his cows and I had stayed behind, I grew bored and decided to walk out to the highest hill on the ranch that was about a mile from the house, to see if I could spot him somewhere out there in the fields. I climbed the hill which had a long, rising slope to the highest point and then dropped off more or less precipitously to the slough below and the field spread out around it. I reached the highest point and let my gaze sweep out as far as the horizon twenty or more miles away and then brought my eyes in closer and closer. There was Peter, lying below me on the edge of the dried-up slough among his foraging cattle, his horse browsing beside him, and at the edge of the spread-out, peacefully chewing animals, a few antelope grazing as well. Peter was sound asleep. The animals were aware of him but unconcerned, as if he were one of them.

Something about this scene so struck me that I backed away down the slope of the hill and hurried back across the field to the ranch house. I did not tell him what I had seen; I did not tell anyone. It had struck me so hard, viscerally, in my soul, that I could not find words for it; I did not understand why I was so moved that for a second I had been unable to breathe, nor why I had hurried away as if I had no right to see what I had seen, as if I was an intruder in this tableau of such calm beauty.

For years I thought of what I had seen, and in another fifteen or more, when I began to write my book about learning to live in nature, I finally decided to tell that story. I began to understand slowly that what I had seen, that picture of great peace and harmony in nature, was the central figure of my entire book. It had been as if I had stepped into a dream, had come in that visionary moment to see the essence of who Peter was. I remember him too, in winter, snow falling on us, in his faded brown canvas jacket ragged at the wrists, his hat pulled low, doing something with his thick fingers, untangling a knot to open a gate, maybe, lifting his head a little to grin at me as I waited, snug in my down-filled jacket, mitts, tuque, and wool scarf, while the animals stood around us, waiting patiently, too, to be let into the shelter of a corral.

I was learning to live around animals. I had to watch out for bulls or stallions if they were about, or, if I was on foot, be careful not to get too close to the herd, as I am a small person and the cattle were huge and, if they became interested in you, might choose to crowd around you, inadvertently crushing and even trampling you. Initially, I didn't know that cougars stalked the coulees, that coyotes might attack — in those first twenty or more years, everyone insisted that no coyotes had ever attacked a human (except for a few incidents in Texas many years earlier) — and so although I saw them all the time, I wasn't afraid of them, and our area apparently had no rattlesnakes except in drought seasons, although they were there to the east and to the west of us.

At the ranch on similar solitary forays I once walked by myself more than a mile north from the house, until I was well into the hills and far from any road, much farther still from any dwelling. My memory is that I had reached a place where in the midst of so many hills, nearly all of the same height with long, easy slopes leading to wide draws between them, I glanced up from my ruminations and saw perhaps a hundred feet away from me a large coyote trotting casually along perpendicular to me and gazing at me over his shoulder. I watched him, not in the least alarmed, as I still believed coyotes didn't attack humans. For some reason, the remnants of an atavistic instinct at work, perhaps, I glanced over my shoulder and saw that the same distance behind me and also trotting perpendicular to me was a second large bushy coyote. At once I understood: They were circling me;

I was prey, or as if I were prey, as I thought they were merely, as Peter always said, animals greatly curious about the comings and goings of people.

But I gasped aloud, I clapped my hands together as noisily as I could. Both animals paused, but they didn't run away. There was nothing around me that I could have used as a weapon, not a long stick — there were no trees or even shrubs more than a foot high — and where I was, no rocks to throw that I was strong enough to lift. I ran; I ran until I had run completely out of breath, and when I stopped because I had to, I did not know where I was in relation to where I had been, because there was no way to tell one hill from another, and though it seemed to me I hadn't run any distance at all, I was as winded as if I had run a very long way. But when I looked around, the coyotes had vanished; they might have been hiding behind other hills, but I couldn't see them, and I kept going straight for home as fast as I could. At the time the experience seemed poetic; I actually wrote a long-ish poem about it that was published. Today, hearing about the rash of cases of people out alone on wilderness trails from Nova Scotia to Alberta who were attacked and killed by them, I marvel once again at my good fortune that they simply lost interest and went away.

Peter did the worrying. Born to this life, he needed nothing from me except the wifely things and, a lot of the time, as long as I was young enough to do it, unskilled labour. I had to drive the trucks or sometimes a tractor, make endless lunches and even more endless thermoses of coffee, chase calves up an alley, open or close gates, sometimes help with the winter feeding of cattle, at his direction ride horses and herd cattle. If I didn't always like the work and wasn't especially good at it, not being athletic and being too small to have much strength or "reach" for awkward jobs that took two people, for many years, although it often frightened me and always exhausted me, I found it endlessly fascinating. In the face of my inability to paint anymore — I had planned to spend

my time on the ranch by returning to what I thought was my true
vocation — and in the excitement and wonder of this foreign
way of life and what it was opening inside me, I was becoming,
instead, an observer, a writer. I've written in earlier chapters of my
increasing understanding of the geological and historical layers of
this land. I also started to see it through the eyes of a rancher. And
a writer.

I bought many books, mostly about the plants that Peter could
identify with ease, and I went with him to three different range
schools given by the local agriculture department people, whose
object was to teach you to recognize a certain number of the plants,
to know their characteristic behaviour, where they might be found,
their protein content in various seasons, and thus their value as feed
for cattle and/or horses. I learned which animals would eat which
plant and in which season, and which wouldn't. One of the first
range schools I attended with Peter was to be held in a field across
the border in the Bears Paw Mountains in Montana. Those tanta-
lizing and wild-looking mountains hovered low along the distant
southern horizon. Just as a few Montana ranchers would come up
to the Canadian schools, a few Canadians would go down to the
American schools. As Peter didn't know the way to the ranch and
fields where this one was to be held, he arranged to follow a couple
of his bachelor friends.

The man leading us in his half-ton drove like the proverbial
bat out of hell on the rough gravel roads; it was all Peter, one of
the best drivers I've ever ridden with, could do to keep up without
having an accident. I had my left arm across the back of the seat
and when we hit an unexpected bump the truck leaped up, as did
I, then crashed down, nearly tearing my arm out of its socket. We
stopped at a crossroads where there was a bar for a quick drink — it
was only about eleven in the morning or maybe even earlier, but,
curious as always about this new life I found myself in, and determined to be game, I made no comment. The woman behind the

bar, tall, strong-looking, and stout, said to me, "What'll yuh have, little lady?" This seemed, at the moment, perfectly natural coming from her, but really, who talks like that? Only people in early Western movies. But I was amused.

But then, I'm a Canadian, and despite the fact that Western Americans and Canadians make their living in the same way, in agricultural enterprises mostly and also in natural resources, notably in oil and gas extraction, the differences between the two cultures seem to be great. The American West is older, of course, and historically more violent than ours. I've heard their relationship with the Aboriginal people was even worse, and it was followed by the range wars between ranchers and settlers (even into the 1950s) over land usage. Canada managed to avoid these wars. However, in one crucial aspect, American history was more progressive. According to the Homestead Act of 1862, American women had the right to free land on the same basis as men did, while according to the Dominion Lands Act of 1872, Canadian women were almost entirely refused the right to free land. Combined with this basic injustice was the striking down of dower rights in 1886, which left Western Canadian women without the basic right of inheritance of their husband's property on his death, and also allowed the husband during his life to dispose of his property as he chose without his wife's agreement. It was out of the latter discovery that my novel *Wild Rose* came into being. Such systemic discrimination against women leaves its marks on the society that grows up within it, and perhaps this helped to explain why the region in which I found myself was so entirely male-oriented, at least in the public arena.

There was only one other woman in the maybe thirty of us taking part in the range school that day and she, although almost exactly my size, was something of a wild woman, a horse-breaker herself. Her husband, who had come separately, and who said he'd been "working colts in the corral," wore his spurs through the whole event, at which the other men looked askance, while some snickered at or commented in low tones about this as mere showing off. Otherwise, they all seemed to get along, and Peter seemed to be accepted, if a bit stiffly, among the men. In any case, there were other Canadian men there for him to talk to, while I was the only Canadian woman.

When at the end of the day we arrived in someone's ranch yard for the de rigueur beef barbecue, three or four of the wives of the other men appeared, but did not come near me and completely ignored the other woman. I couldn't quite muster the courage to approach the wives, feeling sure I would be treated as if I were a Martian, even though we were at the most maybe seventy miles south of our own ranch house. Thus, I went to talk to that other woman; we chatted for quite a while and there was something about the way she spoke, utterly straightforward in a plain but gentle way and without much change in her facial expression — I think now that she was harbouring a steady pain that had perhaps been with her since childhood, although I could only guess what its source might be — that made me like her very much.

She told me about a time when she was a girl out alone in the field on horseback checking her family's cattle, when she was spotted by a crew of convicts from a nearby prison camp who were out fixing fence. One of the convicts leaped on his horse and went after her, she feared to rape her, and she, already on her horse, and not being stupid, rode as fast as she could for home. He chased her all the way to her home ranch. She barely outran him (which means, in that country, most likely that she outrode him) and pulled up and finally turned back to check on him only as she reached the safety of the buildings. She told me other intimate stories in that plain, thoughtful, but faintly puzzled way of hers that made me want to hug her, and to plumb her life for more stories and for other ways of looking at this world in which I'd found myself. In the years since, thinking of her gentle nature,

I know that all the stories of "the true West" are not past, and do not belong only to men.

I wrote my first novel when I was nine. I remember the idea of doing such a thing occurring to me and how very excited I was by the notion, experiencing something far beyond a child's normal excitement over good things, more like the exquisite excitement and wonder of a small child at Christmas. As it had for many children, especially those from a rural world, my reading had far outstripped my personal experience and I thought, at first, that I must be the only child in the entire world who had ever thought of writing a book herself. I knew that a book had to be about something dramatic, even exotic, and set in a faraway place. Accordingly, my novel was set in northern North Dakota, USA, which might as well have been on the moon given that I hadn't been farther than the city of Prince Albert, or else Nipawin, Saskatchewan, where I'd been born, both places within one hundred miles of Melfort, the small farming town in which we then lived.

I decided to write about a kidnapping — I suspect I'd been reading Nancy Drew books, although I've no memory of doing so — and I chose to take my imaginary family, one much like my own, on a driving trip. Only a day or so into the holiday, one of the children, a girl my own age, is kidnapped, but why or by whom is never explained. I don't recall even thinking about that part. The family decides they might as well keep on with their holiday, and when they arrive at the next town, they receive a note from the kidnappers. How I wish I could remember that note. In any case, within the ten pages that made up the entire novel, the child is returned to her family, no harm has been done, and that is the end of that story.

Most of us remember such childhood exploits with a certain amount of sentimental self-love and some tenderness, me included. Chiefly, I remember my tremendous excitement, how hard my heart beat in my chest and how fiercely I concentrated on gripping that pencil, how miraculous my wonderful new endeavour felt. My greatest regret is that, although my mother was equally excited by my initiative and found some red cardboard to make a cover and tied it together with blue wool from her knitting basket, neither of us had any idea what the next step should be. She told me to show it to my teacher, who showed next to no interest, didn't even want to look at it as I held it out to her — it was 1949 in Melfort, Saskatchewan; we had three grades in the room; my teacher was very young, with only a high school education and some bare-bones teacher training. I could only conclude that whatever I had felt, I had been wrong about its significance. After the novel, when I was between ten and twelve, I spent a lot of time walking around with a cheap ruled notebook and a pencil, writing mostly plays, or attempts at plays, as the only ones I'd ever seen were our school Christmas pageants. From then on, aside from my efforts at playwriting that didn't last long, I wrote only what I was asked in school to write. Instead, I turned my efforts to drawing and to visual art. I did not think of being a writer again until I married Peter and went to the ranch to live.

I discovered early on that after having not painted for so many years, a dozen at least, I no longer could. It was not only that I had lost so much craft, but more that I no longer had the desire, that I had lost the ability to give myself completely over to whatever I was working on: a drawing, a painting. Part of my life seemed to have died. I mourned for a while, but then I began to think about writing down all that I was seeing in this fascinating new universe I had moved to. First, I thought about the possibility of writing magazine articles about ranch life and rural culture, not in order to be a journalist — I never thought that far ahead — but because the

creative part of my being had been awakened by ranch and country
life and being in nature again. I didn't dare think that I might be
a *writer*, someone who wrote novels, and I certainly never thought
of writing non-fiction books, because they had never interested me
much, and at that period in my life, when so much change was
going on, they especially didn't interest me.

By this time it was 1978 and I had long since come to the end
of that first year of being constantly with Peter, learning every second of every day. I was now spending many hours by myself. When
I discovered there wouldn't be enough housework to keep me busy
more than an hour or two every morning, I began to go outside. At
the hay farm, I wanted to know what was at the top of the hills to
the north and south of us, and what swam in the river, and what a
certain bird was that I saw every day, and why the rocks scattered
down the hillsides were of so many different kinds. The distances
at the ranch were much longer, and sometimes the cattle kept me
from certain fields, but I was as curious there as I was in the valley
at the hay farm. The atmosphere was different at the ranch, though,
no less surprising and pleasurable, but somehow more *spacious*. I
began to walk the fields, and to think as I walked.

It was only when I began to *not-think* as I walked, that I began
to discover a new dimension in nature, a dimension that, for lack of
a better name, I call visionary; I began to feel the presence of *spirit*
all around me. In my first year of this new life, my great dreaming
had begun. The vast presence and mystery of nature, that endless,
star-pricked sky, the great fields of grass melding into the far horizon, the dreams that took me into another space, the small, edu-
cative visions, plus Peter's teachings about the land, the plants and
animals, the way of life, most of this extended by my own extensive
reading and my pondering on this, together made me into a writer.
I wanted to understand this new world, to find a place for it in my
understanding of human life, and writing about it was the best
way. Understanding it, of course, involved understanding myself.

Strangely, I never thought to try to draw a line between my notion to write a novel at age nine and the excitement that idea engendered in me, and this extraordinary, trans-worldly experience that was filling me, at the age of thirty-eight, with the desire to be a writer. I wouldn't have seen them as connected. It is only now, nearly forty years after my second attempt at writing, that I see the connection. Perhaps, as a mystic would say, there is no *line*, there is only a *state*, and surely that state is, at least in part, one of wonderment at the world, and the place of humans in it.

Article-writing paled very quickly. I wrote in longhand, until one day Peter in his riding boots clomped into the front room of the old frame house at the ranch, shoving open the permanently stuck door, and said to me, "Here." I was sitting on the sofa absorbed in a book and only then noticed he had come in. I looked up: He had brought me a typewriter. Although understanding perfectly well that a pioneer society such as the one I was born into can't do much better in the way of educating its children, I constantly decry the lack of love in that education, and the attitude that either a child could do the work or couldn't. But this was one time my education, which bored me to death a lot of the time (though for two of my four high school years I had a wonderful English teacher, Mr. Harms, and in my fourth year the very fine Mr. Smythe), did me one favour. I had been forced, for reasons I still don't know, as I was in the so-called "academic" stream, to take a course called "business practice" and also typing. Hence, when Peter handed over that typewriter, I could already type like a wiz. This ability that I had heretofore loathed put me miles ahead of many of my fellow novice writers.

I had a world to write about, I was constantly reading the best literature I could find so that I had models and a goal, I knew how to type, I had loads of time as long as Sean was in school and no pressure other than the pressure I put on myself, but that pressure was — well, it's hard to say how immense it was. I was thirty-eight

and thirty-nine and forty; I had no time to lose and so very much
to learn. Trying to think how one began a career as a writer, I supposed that a novel was the place to start. I started writing one, long
since destroyed, and finished it and knew it was terrible. (My subject was the self-destructiveness of some of the young people of the
town near where I lived: drug taking, alcoholism in the very young,
sexual profligacy — or so I was told. What a bad idea that was for
a novel. In the end, my heroine rides her horse off out of the town
heading to Palermo, which she thinks is in South America.)

I recall, after that, trying to think what I should write about
next and toying with the idea of writing a novel about university
life with a single-mom-academic protagonist, completing about
fifty pages before I realized that I couldn't solve the big problem:
How could a novelist manage to give the reader the impression
that she knew all about the life of the protagonist, when only small
selected sections of it were actually written down? How did a writer
manage a sense of continuity? Clearly, I thought, I needed some
instruction. And equally clear to me was the fact that starting out
with a novel was asking far too much of myself. I needed to be
writing short stories — not that I had the faintest idea how to do
that, either.

So I read the new writers everybody was raving about then:
Atwood, Munro. I studied their stories so hard that I could predict
where either writer would go next at a certain juncture in their
story, and how very different they were. I read dozens of other
short-story collections written by the "greats," and I began to get a
feel for how a short story worked. Our doctor's wife at that time was
an Oxford graduate in literature and she gave a one-night-a-week
class for a few weeks to a few of us would-be writers, and I began to
get the idea that maybe — just maybe — I could write. Then the
community college (a process then, not a building or an institution
of the sort we have today) agreed to bring a creative writing teacher
down to us. Through the Saskatchewan Writers' Guild (which, I

hasten to point out, was the first writers' guild in Canada), Caroline
Heath, an incisive, super-smart, highly esteemed critic and editor,
arrived to teach a full-day workshop on short-story writing. That
was the beginning of our relationship that lasted until her too-early
death at only forty-eight. She was my first mentor, teacher, guide,
and eventually, when she began her own publishing house called
Fifth House, my first publisher. Early in those days, maybe around
1979, when I would have been thirty-nine, her interest in my work
(and that of a few other writers she had identified as particularly talented) and her intense support and guidance were a lifeline. Sometimes I felt like a drowning creature that she hauled out of the sea
with her own efforts and brought back to life with her nurturing.

Over the next couple of years, I wrote something like two dozen
short stories; I laboured over them, and rewrote, sometimes as many
as thirty-five times, until they felt right. I doubt I was doing much
to improve the story in question after maybe the tenth rewrite, but
I was learning every minute how to write. Then one morning as
I sat at my (now electric) typewriter to begin a new short story, a
voice said to me, "This is a novel," and even though I told the voice
that it was crazy, that I was not ready yet to write a novel, it simply
insisted, and would not shut up until I acquiesced. That is how my
first novel, Country of the Heart, came about. By this time, Caroline
Heath had started her publishing company, although she wasn't
ready to publish this novel until 1984. In 1985 my short stories
were published as Queen of the Headaches by Coteau Books, and,
astonishingly, were shortlisted for the Governor General's Award. I
say "astonishingly," because they were the first stories I had written
and I couldn't convince myself they were worthy of such an honour.

How very driven I was to write, and this did not improve until
Peter's death in 2007, when I was sixty-six, although after the first
few years I had at least the grace to question my priorities. When
in the mid-nineties I was shortlisted for something like three major
prizes and won none of them (I did win other, less significant

prizes), I could only think that I must have offended the gods with my overweening ambition. But my losses, chastening as they were, only spurred me to try harder, part of me arguing that I should try to live by what I knew to be true, which was that prizes didn't matter. In rare moments I felt the truth of this.

The stages of my education as a writer are very clear to me, although the order in which they came is not. More likely they were all growing at once. I even realized that I needed a subject that I could know intimately. With some reluctance, having imagined a more glamorous universe open to me, I realized that my subject had to be the rural agricultural world of the Great Plains of Canada, and in particular, the women of that world. When I think about this hard-won choice now, I see it as not a choice at all, but as inevitable. It is this subject matter that people think of when they think of my work — this and nature. Probably such choices for writers are always inevitable, whether they think so or not.

As I mentioned earlier, the Nobelist J. M. Coetzee, in a letter to the American writer Paul Auster, noted this about his art:

One can think of a life in art, schematically, in two or perhaps three stages. In the first you find, or pose for yourself, a great question. In the second you labor away at answering it. And then, if you live long enough, you come to the third stage, when the aforesaid great question begins to bore you, and you need to look elsewhere.

David Atwell suggests that Coetzee's "great question" "would be something like, *What script has my history written for me, and how can I rewrite it?*" My own "great question" had to be, *What is a human life worth?* And in particular, *What is a woman's life worth?* My question referred especially to the lives of people in the rural, agricultural world that I was coming to know so well.

My ambition, my willingness to give over my entire life to

learning to be a writer, and then a better writer, and a better one after that, was plaited into my life as a housewife, a ranch wife, Peter's wife. I carried a notebook with me everywhere I went, and whenever Peter got out of the truck or the tractor or off the baler or the feed wagon, I whipped it out and started making note of how certain plants looked in winter and what animals had been around, judging by their scat and their prints in the snow or mud. I tried to look for similes to describe what a herd of Herefords looked like flowing over a broad hill, or antelope skimming the grass; I often carried a well-thumbed book on prairie plants so as to tell one from another and make note of how they changed with the seasons. I watched horses being broken in the corral — pre-horse-whisperer days — and wrote down what I saw; I studied the bulls, mesmerized by their lazy, heavy power, and I studied the men for their unassuming courage in situations that scared the heck out of me, and the women for their brand of courage to keep going day after day in a world that, aside from their children and housekeeping skills, was never built for them. I often thought that my heart would break for the women (who absolutely did not want my empathy, pity, or compassion). Once or twice I felt the same for the men, how they were bound to their lives on the land and with their animals, hard and unrelenting taskmasters as they were. They appeared to accept this preordained life. This world *I* lived in though seemed to me to be the true world, or the real world in microcosm, and I yearned to grasp it wholly, although, in all my thirty-three years there, I never felt that I did.

From the time I made the conscious decision to write about this world, I knew my real challenge would be to make the subject matter interesting to urban people, because that's who the bulk of readers are. Sadly, most urban people have little interest in the lives of rural people. And I was no longer young, and in touch with whatever it was twenty- and thirty-year-olds cared about, and that worried me too. Still, classic novels about the lives of women — Madame

Bovary and Anna Karenina and Hardy's Tess — lived on because the work was so true psychologically. I would have to learn to write *that well* if I wanted an audience.

I mourned my isolation from other writers and from the writing world. But in the end, I know it was my very isolation that made me into the writer I've become, because I wasn't influenced by whatever other writers were talking to each other about, whatever the literary fashions were. I was forced to create my own path. I wasn't distracted by readings or literary events unless I chose to take a few days to drive to the city for them. I was pretty much on my own — nobody dropping in for coffee or a glass of wine, or for a long, chatty walk. Nor did I have a clue what the current gossip was in the writing world, and so lost no time over even the greatest scandals, hearing about them only years later, if at all. I just wrote and read and thought and walked alone, and wrote some more. As a side effect of my isolation, I began to get a reputation as prolific. But the truth is that I wasn't an especially fast writer or an unusually creative one. Despite ranch work and housework and some small work I did in the community, I was fortunate in being able to put in more hours each day, day after day, year after year, than almost any other writer I knew.

When I think back to those days in the late seventies and the eighties, even the nineties of the twentieth century, I wonder how else I might have lived my life. Could I have had a better life if I hadn't been so driven to be a writer? But I know that the work was so tightly interwoven with my own drive to know who I was and who I might be, fed as it was by my encounters in nature, that there was no possible "other" life.

Thus, I read a stream of books, usually four and even (rarely) five at a time, putting one down when I was tiring and picking up another, putting that one down when Peter called me to come and help, either by driving a truck, or by riding with him to bring in a sick cow, or to sort out calves, or to check fences, or to open and close gates in the corral, or else to make coffee and a snack for the few men who were giving him a hand that day. At first I left my writing without looking back, believing that my duty to Peter should always come first, but later I might reply, "Just a minute!" and delay a few minutes. Eventually, I would reply that I'd come as soon as I finished whatever I was doing. Writing had taken over. Peter would often reply, "You keep on with what you're doing. I'll get so-and-so to help me," but, although he never said a word of complaint, I am sure that eventually there was a level where he resented my preoccupation. I can hardly blame him.

For the most part, though, these strands of my life — the writing, the housekeeping, the ranch work — worked together rhythmically, each giving me a break from the other, and each feeding the other. Struggles in my writing life only brought me closer to my spiritual life, which was fed so profoundly by relentless sky, the nightly crowd of unknowable stars, constellations, and galaxies, and the smell of prairie on the ceaseless wind.

6

Old Man On His Back

I became a rancher's wife, I became a writer, I lived a life in nature. I lived under the stars — seeing the stars every single night as you can't see them in the city. I was out in all kinds of weather, heavily bundled in winter, my breath streaming out white in front of me, the sky so brilliant and the snow even brighter so that it hurt my eyes to look, made them run with water. More than once we found ourselves in situations, never entirely by chance, where only Peter's strength and knowledge kept us alive.

Once when we were driving to the ranch from the hay farm, we finally could go no farther because of four-foot, wind-hardened snowbanks across the road. Peter (as women would say, being a man) kept plowing forward, believing, I can only guess, that it would get better at the higher reaches where the road would be windswept clean. Instead, we became thoroughly stuck in this heavy, crusted snow. It was about thirty below Fahrenheit (about −34°C), and miles to the nearest occupied dwelling. Usually, when we became stuck in snow, on Peter's instructions, I just waited in the cab, or kicked at the crusted snow the tires were embedded in while Peter shovelled for the few necessary moments. This time, though, mid-afternoon on a frozen winter Sunday, with a vast, hard, cloudless pale sky above us, no traffic, and miles from an open road, in any event, I realized the seriousness of our situation right away. I had only to look at Peter's determination as he reached into the truck box and pulled out a second shovel, and I started moving snow too.

I did so eagerly, with a kind of shared purpose, because I understood how close we were to freezing to death. All my life, although winter had always been something to fear in the West, I had protected myself from risky situations. I had been raised with such caution, taught to be always careful because I was a girl, and a small, inexperienced one. As a child I had dared nothing, because I thought the world belonged to others, never to me. Now I was finding the side of myself I had never known. I was finding strengths I'd been unaware of. That instant of fear when I realized our dire situation passed at once into a kind of inarticulate joy that even now I marvel at.

The bitter winters were followed by sweltering summers. In summer heat, carrying out coffee or lemonade in hundred-plus-degree temperatures (104°F is 40°C) and sitting with Peter in the cleared patch of cut alfalfa while insects buzzed around and there was no other sound except maybe the faint drone of a neighbour's swather a mile or more away, I inhaled the delicious fragrance of the hay, both cut and standing, filling my nostrils while little ground-nesting birds flittered cheerily and swooped around us. I remember those endless summer days when the sun was up by five and darkness didn't come until ten at night, and it seemed, somehow, that the sun didn't ever fully set, that the sky glowed faintly all through the short northern night. The nights were magical and if for some reason you rose in the dark, you just held your breath for the beauty of it.

Am I imagining the pleasure of that world? The wonder? The ecstasy, even? I do not think so; my heart cracks for what I have lost, even given the travails that I also struggled with there.

Peter and I often rode together in the early years, he giving me advice about how to ride a horse, what to do and what not to do, but more often I had to draw it out of him, because he belonged to what I privately thought was an idiotic school of thought which was that if you do it wrong long enough, you'll eventually figure out the right way yourself. How much time did he think I had? I was already thirty-six and not exactly in love with horses or riding, or with chasing cows. Yet in those days we never went out merely to ride; every single trip out from the corral was to do a job: to pick up a sick cow or calf and move it or them back to the corrals for doctoring or a trip to the vet, to move the bulls to where the cows were, to move cattle from one field to another, to separate the steers and bring them in, or to fix fence (although then we usually went in the old truck that served for fencing only and that rarely went on a road anymore). Riding for pleasure didn't exist. Even when we had visitors who wanted to ride, Peter would make good use of them, and sometimes, because they were actually working whether they knew it or not, they got more riding than they'd bargained for.

And yet, one of my proudest moments as a wife came when one day we were riding side by side, heading back to the barn, and our horses were being driven mad by horseflies and mosquitoes, so much so that mine was doing something the cowboys called "crow-hopping," that is, jumping on all fours. (He was also swinging his head and twisting just a bit, although hardly to the degree of rodeo saddle-bronc twisting.) He couldn't be stopped from this behaviour, which was why we were heading back — to spray them with horse insect repellent — and I, in order to stay on the horse, was laughing and standing and swinging in my stirrups. Peter glanced over at me and, seeing this, beamed in surprise and pleasure and said, "Now you're riding!"

It could not be said of me that when it came to riding horses I was a natural.

Nonetheless, I got so that I enjoyed riding most of the time, although sometimes I got too tired, and still I had to sit on that horse and keep going. Sometimes I found myself wondering if I had failed to understand something about the contract Peter and I had made. Was I to be a hired hand, and one who, because of my inexperience, always took the last place if anybody more experienced came along? More than once I pointed out to him that at least our hired man got paid. When I told people that even the cattle dog had higher rank than I did, they thought I was joking. But any rancher will tell you how invaluable a well-trained, smart cattle dog is. I could only pity a wife who was *that* loyal. But although I sometimes fumed and sometimes complained out loud and wondered what I'd spent all those years at university for, if this was how I was going to spend my life, I was so stimulated by what I was seeing, and so thrilled that, for the first time since I was a child, I had free time to spend on my own, I just did what was asked of me. And of course I held rank in the house and made a special effort to become a good cook, something during my first marriage I had never had time to concentrate on and had always wanted to achieve. Often, when Sean became old enough to drive and was on his way to the ranch for a long weekend, I would knock myself out in the kitchen, sometimes cooking a turkey with stuffing and all the other dishes usually reserved for Christmas dinners, just so he would know how much he was loved, how very happy I was to see him.

My pleasures with Peter were simple and invariably involved the land around us. When he had time off, or wanted to celebrate my birthday, for instance, he would take me on his motorcycle into a field I wanted to see with him — not by myself — where we could sit on rocks and study the flora and the fauna and talk about the sky, or the deer in the coulee behind us, or where we just sat in silence and gazed around in quiet pleasure. Or else we would get in the truck and he would drive us to some far-distant, seldom-travelled road nobody else was on where we could drive slowly and take in the countryside in an especially beautiful part of the country. Or we would go cross-country on trails he had learned about as a boy trailing cattle to the railway or to a sale ring with his father that were far from any highway or even a ranch yard. He knew that I liked nothing better than to be out in the landscape, going slowly or not moving at all, just looking at it, trying to get the feel of it, with nothing required of me but to look and look and look, to smell the air and the many scents always riding on it, to feel it on my skin. The same was true of him, and of who knows how many other ranching men who would keep this love well hidden from others. Over the years we drove everywhere, to distant landmarks, or to towns via narrow dirt back roads you wouldn't go near if they were wet, or in winter when they would be buried under snow and ice. Every one of these forays was material for my writing, not just because I became more familiar with the landscape in which I lived, but also because there was so much opportunity to notice details about the animals who lived there and about the trees, plants, and the general lay of the land, all of which I needed to know to be able to write authentically.

One of our favourite drives, although we didn't do it very often, was to aim for Medicine Hat, Alberta, but to go west and then north to Cypress Hills Park on the Saskatchewan side, drive through the park, steadily climbing, and at the top of the hills, keep on heading west past the far park boundary, onto ranchers' land on trails that were marked with the sign IMPASSABLE WHEN WET and which were taken very seriously by even the most local of the local men (gumbo again, and not a speck of gravel). We would pass historic Fort Walsh, nestled in its beautiful green valley with the forest behind and the creek running by that in spring might be a roaring cataract, take the road above it that continued west across the high yellow prairie, drop down into a deep, long, partially treed valley, and move on slowly through grassy ranchland, and finally into Cypress Hills Park on the Alberta side, go through the resort village of Elkwater, drive north on a paved road until, finally, a couple of hours after we'd first driven into the park, we would meet the Trans-Canada Highway and head east again into Medicine Hat. It took a lot longer to go that way, but when we did it, the pleasure of it always seemed to us to be well worth the extra time.

We didn't talk much on these drives, Peter not being a loquacious person at the best of times, and I was silenced by the beauty we were driving through. Sometimes Peter would tell me a story about the people who had once owned the land we were passing by, or remark on the condition of the fields and corrals. As it might from any rural man, new farm machinery always brought a comment too. But when I think back on our years of driving together, I don't really remember a single conversation. We travelled comfortably side by side, each lost in our own thoughts, our eyes turned to the landscape outside the truck windows, and at such moments I believe we were thinking much the same thoughts. Chiefly, though, the emotion we shared was sheer, deep-seated pleasure.

Peter and I never quarrelled, chiefly because Peter couldn't stand quarrelling, would leave the house, saddle his horse, and ride through the fields until he figured the quarrel had dissipated — not resolved, never resolved. I wanted to talk everything through, but what that in practice meant was that I talked and he mostly didn't listen, although pretending to, and didn't reply. You can well imagine that by the end of our first year together I gave up completely the urban-academic method of resolving differences as a waste of my time. If I wanted to get my own way about this or that, I was going to have to be a lot cagier about it. But Peter was no dummy, and being cagier often didn't work either.

We had our difficulties, but they seem unimportant now: his belief in his ability to read the character of others, which I privately thought was abysmal; my increasing intolerance for the less charming of local practices, to which he was required to continue to pay homage, despite his knowing better. Sometimes I lost patience; I grew angry; I refused to participate. Sometimes he buried himself in his work. But don't all couples find ways to overcome the inevitable frictions? I retreated into nature, and he wandered off to do whatever it was he did when I wasn't around. In any event, it was a community where men and women for the most part kept their roles separate. But I was also becoming a writer, for which a certain distance was necessary. I often wonder if my increasing role as an observer set me apart from other people.

As Peter aged, though he never made more than a brief mention of his concerns to me, he began to think about what would become of his ranch. (The hay farm wasn't at issue: We had come a long way since the 1886 striking down of Western women's dower rights that left abandoned farm wives penniless and helpless. Now, should Peter die first, my rights to the hay farm were legally assured.) He had no direct heir; despite all the time Sean spent with us, and his ability to ride horses and understand the basics about cattle and the land, he had no desire to become a rancher. And Peter silently harboured a different, bigger dream. He was afraid that if he simply

put the land up for sale it would be sold off piecemeal, as few people could have afforded to buy the whole place outright, most of
which was Crown land anyway — that is, land belonging to the
government of Saskatchewan and leased to the Butala family for an
extended period, with the lease renewed periodically until in nearly
everyone's eyes it was Butala land. He had managed the ranch so
that the grass was in excellent condition, and such was the nature
of his heart that he couldn't bear to see the place destroyed as one
grassy whole, not to mention that a good part of its value for conservation purposes was the fact that it was such a large intact area.

He wanted to find a conservation organization that would buy
the ranch and acquire, along with the native prairie that he owned,
the lease as well, so that the whole miraculous place could be kept
in one piece. Together, that is what we set out to do, and as I always
point out to people, it was Peter's initiative. If I had wanted to do
this and he hadn't, it would never have happened, despite my name
on the deeds; with my name on the deeds and my dower rights he
could not do it without my assent. But I was with him 100 percent
right from the moment he declared this to be his desire. His parents
were dead by then, and his sisters did not object, were even, I think,
rather proud of him, and in the end, pleased with his innovative
and creative decision. Suffice it to say that this took a long time,
several years, to become fact, and the organization in question was
the Nature Conservancy of Canada, who in 1996 became the owners of both the deeded land we donated to them and the remainder
that they purchased, along with control of the government lease.

It was heartbreaking to both of us to have to give up the place,
I am sure much more to Peter than to me, but he was never one to
show his feelings if he could help it. He was caught up in the excitement (and the drudgery of the endless legal work) of being the first
to do such a thing in the Province of Saskatchewan — that is, with
an area of such size — and in the many meetings he had to attend,
and the applause he received, even though most of his neighbours

were aggrieved. They had wanted access to his lease and/or to buy his deeded property on his retirement; worse, he had brought the much-dreaded environmentalists right into the neighbourhood.

Nowadays, when all I see of the ranch is good photographs online, I can't look too hard or for too long, because it hurts too much. The beauty of the place takes away everyone's breath: the long, seemingly endless acres of slowly rolling, grass-covered hills, and the way the grass captures the light, at sunset turning rose and pink, at dawn turning to gold, often during the day dissolving into hazy aqua or green outlines against the horizon; miles of grass, backed by layers and different shades of blue-green and tan, pale yellow or sage, into the distant sky. Standing on one of the high hills, you can feel as if you have reached the top of the world. This endless Eden is too much for a single person to encompass. It renders everyone who cares about nature speechless. No wonder Peter had his heart — no, every cell of his body — set on saving it for others, for future generations. No wonder any objections had zero effect on him. He was in the grip of a vision.

The people who worked for the Nature Conservancy of Canada as well as their board members, as far as I could tell, fell in love with the place too, and put their considerable brains and vast expertise to work to enact the vision Peter had. We all agreed that in time the true plains buffalo should be brought back home to again inhabit the land they had come from. In the early 2000s, a herd of twenty-five males and twenty-five females was donated from Elk Island National Park in northeast Alberta. They were the descendants of the last remnants of the original herds of the plains, at peak as many as 60 million in number, rescued by a couple of Montana ranchers and purchased by the Canadian government about a hundred years before our project. They were the real thing, their biological name being *Bison bison bison* — genus, species, subspeci (the only other subspecies is wood bison). In later years, Peter u to drive out to the ranch by himself and sit in his unobtrus parked truck, and watch them for hours as they went about their wild business. He would come back to the hay farm and tell me excitedly all about their habits, the way they moved and slept and generally behaved, and how this was different from the habits of cattle he knew so well.

All of us — the nature conservancy and its experts, Peter and I, and the major donors to the project — wanted to preserve the native prairie, and so it was agreed that the 1,200 acres of the 13,108 that made up the Butala ranch, that had been broken by settlers and that Peter usually had cropped by a neighbour, would be returned to their original state. To restore native prairie isn't very easy either, and took considerable effort. Unexpectedly, oil companies knew something about how to do that, because many of their lease agreements required that they return any disturbed land back to its native condition, and they employed people who knew how. But we knew that the seeds for the original prairie had to come from a place very near to the land being reseeded so that the composition of the seeds and the soil they had grown in, as well as the weather conditions and characteristic amount of moisture, would be comparable. It wasn't very long before this came about; the reseeding was a stunning success, and when we first saw the newly grassed fields a year later, Peter and I just stood there grinning in delight and surprise. The first year, though, the grass came in at nearly four feet high, causing us to scratch our heads in puzzlement, but the scientists explained that in time, the new grass would slowly revert to, at most, the foot-high grass characteristic of the mixed-grass prairie around it. As predicted, this came to pass.

The third major initiative that all parties agreed on was that the invader species of plants (plants not native to that particular prairie ecosystem) would be removed, although at that stage my impression was that nobody was sure precisely how to do that. In our case, new clover was a problem, as well as crested wheatgrass from

WHERE I LIVE NOW

Siberia, which had been introduced back in the 1920s by grazing specialists as preferable to the native prairie grass. They saw it as hardier and more nutritious. It certainly turned out to be hardier. Now it was taking over, crowding out the original prairie. A University of Alberta scientist brought in a team and carried out experiments to determine which of the three usual methods worked best: early heavy grazing, fire, or plowing. It took a while to do this, but the result was, I was told, that, in that situation, early heavy grazing was the best way of killing off the unwanted invaders.

There was no end to the excitement in that five-year period when so much was going on and people were coming from all over the country to see the Old Man On His Back Prairie and Heritage Conservation Area, now called verbally, strictly for ease, the Old Man On His Back Ranch (or OMB) and sometimes even the Butala ranch. As I write this, I am making preparations to attend the twentieth-anniversary celebration of its establishment. I think it will be a sad affair for me, as well as a joyous one, not just because Peter won't be there, but because most of the original participants in this glorious project — who remember how exciting it was, how thrilled we all were, how devoted to the endeavour — will not be there, having retired or moved on to other work, and in one significant case, sadly, died.

Once the contracts were signed and the Nature Conservancy of Canada became manager and owner, we kept on ranching for another six years, and held our herd dispersal sale in 2001, although by then Peter had cut back the herd bit by bit so that it was a small sale. Still, he was so devastated by what it represented that had to persuade him to attend it. He had only six years after th good years when he kept an eye on the place and was the off tour-giver, guide, and interpreter (how he relished that job), and we could finally get away to travel, sailing around Orkney and the Shetlands, even all the way to mythic Fair Isle in the North Sea (how he loved sailing!), with our biggest trip together being six weeks away in Hawaii, New Zealand, Australia, and Fiji. I have always been grateful he was well enough for that trip, the fulfillment of a dream he had held for many years.

During this period when we were more or less retired and had begun travelling, but before that last Australian trip, Peter, with great curiosity, entered my world. We had already been to a number of productions in which my actor-writer son, Sean Hoy, had had roles. Peter had viewed them with great interest rather than the bored patience I had expected. We often drove a hundred miles into Swift Current to see productions, music or theatre, brought in by the local arts council, then drove the hundred miles back home. At one of the first of these we attended, the actors had mimed driving in what we would have called a "ground blizzard" (when a strong but low, driving, snow-laden wind keeps you from seeing the road except in glimpses now and then). To do this, two sets of actors with one actor at each end of long flexible strips of white cloth twisted, rippled, and flapped them so that it mimicked exactly what the road would look like to a driver. Peter, apparently never before having seen what professional stage effects can do, said, out loud, in amazement, "T'hell!"

Travelling around the world was thrilling, and we lapped up every new sight, every mode of travel — ever the technology lover, Peter especially couldn't get over the high-tech cross-country buses we took in Mexico from Mexico City or Guadalajara to San Miguel de Allende, claiming there was no such thing in Canada — and every new country. After our yachting excursion in the North Sea and a number of other trips, he decided he wanted most to see where his Slovak father had come from; he wanted to know something about his ancestors. He didn't mention Ireland, his mother's ancestral home as it was my mother's, but I feel sure we would have gone there to seek out the church and graveyard if nothing else, if he had lived longer. (After he was gone, I went twice by myself to Ireland and, with the help of some wonderful Irish people, found the ancestral home and land and graveyard.) Slovakia, however, turned out to be perhaps the most fascinating of all our trips, surprisingly so to me, who had expected nothing much of interest to myself and was doing it mostly to support my husband in his wish to see where he had come from.

This impulse of Peter's to find his father's village was and is anything but unusual on the Canadian prairies. So very many immigrants, well over a million, came from Europe around a hundred years ago or even sooner, most of them with children, and none of the original settlers, or almost none, was ever able to return for even a visit. My impression is that most of them — once the early hardship had lessened — had no desire to return, finding that, eventually, their lives in Canada were so very much better. There was no vicious oppression or torture, no constant war, free education for their children, and plenty of land for all. Peter's father and his uncles were among those who seemed to hold no desire to return. But the next generation feels very differently, and once they have reached middle age, and assuming they are prosperous enough, many of them are eager to see their true homeland.

Our adventures in Slovakia — we took the ten-hour trip between Prague and Košice by train in order to see as much countryside as possible — I described in my non-fiction book *Lilac Moon: Dreaming of the Real West*. In eastern Slovakia then, tourists were a rarity — almost nobody spoke English — so we had to buy small Slovak-English dictionaries and use our wits and a tourist guidebook to get from A to B. My one regret about that trip was that I couldn't persuade Peter to take a local bus from Košice up north to the tiny village Andy Warhol's family came from and where there a cache of Warhol's work I was dying to see.

We had a bit of wonderful good luck in that when we vi

the archaeological dig in the centre of Košice where the original city dating back to the thirteenth century was being excavated, a young male guide with perfect English befriended us and, because we couldn't, found the village on an old map. (It had been destroyed by the Communists twenty or so years earlier, and its inhabitants, who had been told this was to make a pristine watershed area for a dam called Starina that was then built nearby, were moved elsewhere.) Then in his small car he took us and another backpacking tourist, a young Englishwoman he had met the night before in a tavern, out into the countryside east of Košice to find it.

What an adventure that was, seeing the green and fruitful countryside, the tininess of the usually sloping fields — we were in the Carpathian Mountains — compared to the size we Canadians were used to, feeling the steady humidity, and marvelling at the bountiful green forest we trekked through. Pears grew there! The spiders were enormous, furry, and bright yellow! The small crumbling castles on the hills above were a delight. We could hardly believe Peter's father could have left such a paradise, but thinking of the history he had left, and with the First World War about to start, we couldn't blame him.

Then, after certain misdirections and errors, there it was, what was left of the village — nothing, it turned out. But even Communists couldn't move the graveyard. It and the small ceremonial building placed there by the villagers after their dispersal were all that was left. The graveyard was full of Butalas, but sadly the high humidity had left many of the grave markers, especially if made of iron, unreadable, or, if of wood, decayed. We stayed a couple of hours while Peter, moved beyond speaking, the look on his face not describable, dug in the thick green grass, scraped off headstone surfaces, and searched for his ancestral past. We spent another week in e Slovak Republic, but after the graveyard, there could be noth- but anticlimax.

As I've written, Peter wasn't good at talking about his feelings, and I read the importance of this trip to him in the way he held his face and from what I saw in his eyes. I have tried to extrapolate from my own moments driving around the lake district of Northern Ireland and staring at the house, still in use, that my great-grandfather had grown up in, what it was Peter might have been feeling. But I couldn't do it; the two experiences were too dissimilar — he finding his own father's past and I having to go back much farther than that to a man I never in my life saw, about whom I knew only stories, none flattering, although sometimes funny. I was fascinated but not moved; Peter was profoundly moved, and did not want to leave. He told me he had been searching, although fruitlessly, for his grandfather's grave. He was diligent in that search, and I thought it was as if all his life he had been floating and wanted to find an anchor, and thought that in his grandfather's grave he would find it.

This was touching to me, although also puzzling, until I remembered that on my father's side I am deeply proud to say that we are Acadians and can trace our family to the arrival on these shores of the first ancestor in 1647. Once I understood this, some yearning dropped away from me. I felt that — despite my failed struggles to become bilingual, and my not having lived in a French community since I was a small child, and never among Acadians — I knew who I was; I know who I am. Peter's desire to find his grandfather's grave took on a deeper meaning.

But many cultures practice ancestor worship, or something close to worship; those are people who have stayed for many generations in the same place. In the Canadian West it is commonplace, even seemingly de rigueur, to make that trip back to the ancestral home, proving, it seems to me, the universality of that desire to know where one comes from and thus, in some barely explainable sense, who one is. It is a craving of the human soul.

So we went to Slovakia, we found his paternal family's bu‑ site, we went back home again, and he did not talk about it. also oddly, he was determined to preserve the ranch his fathe uncles had created in this new country, having arrived penniless; he was almost completely invested in his identity as the man who had done this, or who would do it, even though his name would not be on it. He bowed to the earlier claim of the Indigenous name, the Old Man On His Back Plateau. He experienced no grief over this, saying, "It is bigger than that," meaning that the project was bigger than his family name. Of course, in the interpretative centre his and his sisters' names are prominent, and there is also a stone memorial to him out on the land. It may be, it occurs to me, that his land and his devotion to it took the place of the natural son he never had, the one who would have carried on the Butala name. As for his father, who died only months after our marriage, I didn't know him well enough to have a sense of how he would have felt about Peter's endeavour, although I do know that he was very proud of him. "I never thought," I once heard him say, gazing admiringly at Peter from across the room, "that I would have such a son!"

It was remarkable that Peter and I survived together for over thirty-one years, especially in the face of predictions that it wouldn't last a year. Even though I came from a family of five girls ("Your poor father," people sometimes said), and even though I'd been married before, men had always been a mystery to me, as I was never raised with brothers. It took us a long time together before he began to be demystified. But that is true, I suppose, of all marriages.

As well, moving from the culturally forward-looking univerity community into a small society where women were definitely ond-class citizens, being reduced to the silent helpmate in pub ircumstances was a challenge for me. I survived only because was proud of me and treated me with respect, so that in his presence the other men were usually not dismissive of me. Over time we found a way to meld our separate and often contradictory worlds, because, in the end, we shared the same values. If he had not been stricken with illness and died too young at only seventy-two, we would have continued to love one another.

As it does for most couples, what we shared in the beginning transformed as the years passed. His sudden, unexpected attraction to me that I didn't take very seriously and my slower attraction to him began to deepen as we learned to know each other better, and bit by bit, he let slip stories of his own past, and I did the same for him. Then, as we both aged, and I slowly withdrew from most active participation in the ranching work, and he had to examine some of his unacknowledged assumptions —- chiefly that I, a five-foot-tall, college-educated non-athlete would be made into a tobacco-chewing, horse-breaking cowgirl, or even a silent, hard-working, acquiescent partner who was always a rank below him — we stepped back a little from our early years of marriage and reconsidered. I had learned so very much from him, had learned to deeply value rural life through his experience and tutelage, whether planned by him or not, and he had grown in sophistication and shed some of his youthful notions about life. We had learned some boundaries that there would be no crossing, even while we had each moved some distance from the people we were when we married.

But at the end, as he lay dying and I stood beside him, my hand on his face, in an unspoken communication that was private between us, it was at last clear to us both that we had become linked together forever in our souls. I see this connection now as something larger, richer, and deeper than romantic love, and I am the more grateful for it.

3

HOME

Sharon and Boots circa 1978.

7

A Place of My Own

O ver the years, given the statistics of women surviving men, I had often asked myself, if I had to leave the country, where would I go to live? With Peter's death the question had suddenly become real, had taken on urgency, and in my frozen state I had no answer. People said to me politely, carefully, "I suppose you'll buy a house in Eastend and live there?" But I didn't want to spend the rest of my life by myself in Eastend, because, as I have said, from there you could drive a hundred miles in any direction and you still wouldn't be anywhere. If that had once seemed intriguing to me — to be "not anywhere" — with Peter's death and my resulting confusion and inability to make decisions, I knew only that such isolation would not be good for me emotionally.

Others said, "You'll be going back to Saskatoon, of course

I would nod in polite agreement, because for many years I had suspected that if anything happened to Peter I would probably go back to where I had come from. But I had arbitrarily chosen to answer "Saskatoon" when people asked where I was from. In truth, I had no hometown, having come from "the bush" south, through three small towns where I'd gone from grade one through grade seven. It was too hard to explain, and not having a hometown seemed to discomfit the questioner, as if it were the same as saying I was a homeless person. Or perhaps the questioner suspected me of lying, and obviously for reasons that had to be disreputable. So I learned to answer "Saskatoon," because, by the time I married Peter, I had spent the longest period of my life there, and because it saved me certain kinds of speculation as to who I was and what might be expected of me. But I had no ancestral home anywhere in Canada, no farm I could point to as the place I'd been raised as both my parents had been able to do, no fixed location even in Saskatoon that I could call home and mean it. Still I had lived there long enough, had had so many formative experiences there, as to feel fully myself when I was there, as I did not anywhere else other than on the hay farm with Peter. I suppose that is one definition, or an important part of one, of home.

But I had no close family members in Saskatoon; even many of my best friends had moved on, even Sean and his family had moved to Calgary, and housing prices had zoomed upward in the year of Peter's death so that it now looked too expensive. If I no longer had any choice but to go to a city, my first choice was Vancouver, but it was priced so ridiculously high that you had to be either very young and willing to live cheaply, or else very rich to get into the housing market there. My two remaining sisters (Sheila died in 1998 breast cancer, and Kathleen in 2014, also of cancer) suggested move to the small coastal British Columbia community where lived, and even though being close to family again had huge those coastal communities felt too isolated to me now. Now that the decision about where to live was mine alone, I swore I'd never live more than two hours from a major airport ever again, or from movie houses showing first-run movies, or from a theatre that staged plays regularly, or from where there were regular chamber music concerts. I see now that I was searching for a place I could call home, but I couldn't find one that had all the necessary components (not that I had ever articulated what those components were) that would allow me to feel, once again, "fully myself."

A few others said, "I guess it will be Calgary now," perhaps thinking that as I was a writer, I belonged in a city, and the closest big city (1.2 million) was indeed Calgary. But for years I'd heard nothing good about it: the dense traffic and belligerent drivers, the intense competitiveness and excessive youthfulness, the super-right-wing tendencies, the way it was Americanized (through oil), the hordes of arrogant, self-indulgent nouveau riche. It was the polar opposite of Eastend, in other words. This judgement, I knew, could be partly attributed to rural people's natural dislike of any city. But Calgary was too big, too urban; even with Sean there it scared me. Where did I find the courage, then, to choose it?

In the end, I left almost everything behind when I moved to Calgary. I left behind nearly all our furniture, and except for a storage locker in Swift Current loaded mostly with books that I couldn't part with, I somehow managed to rid myself of thirty-three years of household objects. I brought a few things with me to Calgary because it would be easier to dispose of them in the city than in a rural community with few agencies for the homeless or the very poor. Some items I brought that I thought I would need turned out to be useless to me in my new life, and eventually I gave them away, the best example being during the aftermath of the great flood of 2013, when I stuffed four large plastic garbage bags with bedding and gave them to a flood-reli drive. Starting again cleanly was turning out to be what I m wanted to do.

Perhaps I felt that such a thing would come in the natural course of living. Perhaps I thought I could simply shake off all those years as if they had never happened, and emerge new to start another new life, as I had once abandoned my career, friends, and family to join Peter on his ranch.

I could not take the land with me — I would deal with that grief later — but I would take a few symbolic remnants of it. I took one buffalo horn, actually the casing thereof, that I had myself found and dug out of the prairie and that I prized as a connection to the heroic past, and a small chunk of the backbone of a cow that was rough-surfaced and stained a dark brown-gold with age and that was to me beautiful art; I took a fossilized piece of fish that either Peter or I had found in the river, one side of which still glimmered purple, green, and blue; I took a few scrapers or flakes I had picked up in the early days, before I developed my own protocol about what I might pick up and what had to stay where it was, that had fluted edges cut by a First Nations person a hundred or a thousand years ago; I prized a large red sandstone scraper I had first found in the field and that represented a place where spirit had spoken to me. I took also — although I can't find it now — the small white skull with the delicate white antlers of a young deer that I nearly tripped over one day in the field. I had held it in my hands in awe at its grace, feeling blessed at having found it. Then I had looked up and counted twenty-two deer, motionless and silent, gazing down at me from the ridge. I brought with me the eagle feather in its carved box that was given me by a First Nations person after Peter's funeral and sometime after an honour song had been sung for him. I gathered what I was afraid would be my last bouquet of pasture sage to put on my desk once I was settled in the city, where it was to fill the room with the blessed, muted, yet pungent scent of Canadian prairie.

I began slowly to understand that my life as a householder was er. I meant by "householder" a woman who had been married way or another for most of her adult life and who had boxes and boxes of accumulated papers, objects, photos, family heirlooms, most of which would have to be thrown away. Being a householder meant having maybe three sets of dishes instead of one: the every-day dishes, the better dishes, and the used-at-Christmas-and-major-celebrations-only dishes, plus battered pots and pans left from my first marriage, plus my usual ill-matching ones and a few glamorous new ones. I would have to strip my housewife's equipment to a basic few things, as if I were a tinker now, or an old-fashioned gypsy living in a caravan.

I would not live in a single house again, so I would not need the lawnmower or the snow shovels or the garden hoses, not even that one that didn't leak. Nor the bluebird houses Peter had attached to the fence posts around our yard, nor my many flower pots of different sizes, nor the large red clay sunburst plaque that I brought from Rome that we'd hung on the outside wall by the back door. A householder has a backlog of things connected to an entire home, not just a house, to times when the kids were young, and to various long-dead pets and, in our case, to the ranching life; I no longer had a home in the old sense of the word. To even think this thought, that I no longer had a *home*, was frightening, but held hints of ex-hilarating possibility, like faint tinges of colour on the far horizon. I might even, in some ways, have felt relieved. Without all those objects I could now really start a new life.

I went even farther and surprised even myself by dropping my membership to the political party that had been my great hope since I was nineteen years old. It was not that I no longer believed in what the party stood for, but that I was starting over, for the third time in my life. I needed to be rid of settled things, defining things, things that entangled me in small, closed worlds. I told almost no-body when I was going, let alone my destination. I said good-bye to my friends, mostly people new to the community who generously put on a small farewell supper. Although people must have know that for months now I had been trying to clean the place of t detritus of so many years of Butala life, and although the assumption was that I was getting ready to sell and leave, I told only two or three local ranching woman-friends of my plans, but not the date I would go. If I thought I was almost invisible as a determinedly independent writer, as a widow I was even more so. Sometimes, when I could think at all, it astonished me how the circle of community life continued on all around me, closing slowly and inexorably to leave me on the outside, while I still stood there, still living and breathing. Often it felt as if I had never been there.

I chose Calgary, even though I had said it was the last place on earth I wanted to go to, because Sean and his wife and children lived there. Of course, I did not think that it was by any means my final destination. With my beloved son's help, I rented that small dark apartment not far from where he and his family lived, and eventually, in late October 2008, I moved in. Of that initial period, other than the constant help Sean willingly gave me, one of my happiest moments in years came the night within the first few days of my arrival when there was a knock on my door and Sean, his wife, Carol, and my two grandchildren filed in, having come to help me put furniture — most of it newly bought — and various belongings into place in my new, if temporary, home. Family at last, joined with me in a family endeavour, after so many years of long-distance communication. This was the first and most blessed boon of my move.

I told myself that in the city I would belong as myself now. In fact, in my first two years in Calgary, apart from the constant loneliness and my rather dismal surroundings, and despite the ongoing hair-clothing-makeup crisis, I was otherwise immersed in city activity: art galleries, museums, film after film after film, nearly as many plays, chamber music concerts, occasionally the opera, and once in a while the symphony or a choral performance, lectures at the university, and especially public readings by writers from around the country. I went home from this sophisticated life to my dingy apartment, a fact that my friends were increasingly pointing out.

Something was wrong, but I ignored it. Instead, I was taking t'ai chi classes, yoga classes, fitness classes. Anything to distract myself.

Life in the city, I was finding, was an unending education: I had for nearly thirty-five years lived in an area so remote it was possible to drive on secondary highways for two hours in any direction without meeting or passing another vehicle, and now I was routinely driving down busy, fast freeways, white-knuckling it to the bookstore I had longed for for so many years, and in despair finally learning to take the LRT downtown and back because of the impossibility of finding parking there. I hadn't parallel-parked since the late sixties and used to joke with people that I'd married Peter because ranchers had lots of room to park. It wasn't just the continuous problem that merely getting from A to B was becoming for me, but that daily life in the city, it seemed to me, was one challenge after another. I had lost the courage for life I had developed in the country. For a city newcomer like me, neither young nor daring, every day is made of difficulties, buying your breakfast cereal or a new pair of shoes, getting your glasses fixed or going to a friend's house to visit. And any widow will tell you that there is a limit to how much help she can ask of her grown children. Every day I fought with myself about staying or going, but I never knew where I should go, and so I kept on with my relentless activity, my frenetic effort to have at all costs what for thirty-three years I had done without.

I often took public transportation and more than once was treated to a close-up view of the underside of city life: an exchange of drugs (powdered white stuff in a plastic baggie) for money between dealer and client, a perfectly ordinary-looking young man on a downtown street that everybody else on the street seemed blind to; the strange, often disheartening and sometimes frightening li vignettes that felt as if they had come out of Dostoevsky or perhaps Tolstoy, which by virtue of my age and invisibility (and writerly curiosity) I saw from and on the LRT; the enormous differences in wealth that shocked me beyond words. I felt as if I had skipped into a modern Henry James novel. There were rows of mansions just one block off a busy street virtually everywhere I went. Nobody in the entire city drove a car cheaper than a Lexus or an Acura, a BMW or a Mercedes (something that in my day, growing up in Saskatoon, we thought only happened in Los Angeles). It is competitive wealth, my clever but much calmer friends said. I was discovering that you do not understand what real wealth is until you live in an oil-and-gas-based city.

At moments of uncertainty and bewilderment about my new life, I would remember my mother's father, our dear grandfather, as an old man, sitting in his armchair in the living room smoking his pipe with the radio on the table with the barley twist legs beside him, listening to the news, shifting only to take out his pipe to knock out the ashes, or to recross his legs, while our grandmother moved quietly about the spotless kitchen or sat across from him on the sofa, the two of them listening to the news again, and then again, all day long. Their lives had seemed so long and hard to me that I thought when I was a child and a young woman they needed only rest. But, looking back, I think they were in their late seventies, not a lot older than I am now, and they both lived until about ninety and died in nursing homes. I think they were listening to the news all day as a substitute for being in life. I wanted desperately not to be like them in their last years, but to be *in* life.

Occasionally, lying in bed sleepless, I would wonder what was going to become of me. Could I go on like this, living from day to day, for twenty years? What would I do if and when my health and vigour began to fail? How would I fill my endless days? A terror would grip me in the darkness. I would clutch the bedclothes, sweat breaking out over my body; I would gasp for air, seeing in front of me the abyss, the one that said, You are nobody now, you have no life and never will again. It is an astonishing, terrifying truth that so easily one can go from living a meaningful life to feeling utter displacement from the human community. Nothing can prepare you for this. But you can overcome it in time.

Very late one night, when I couldn't sleep and my mind was drifting, anchorless, I slowly sank into the ambience of my rural and small-town childhood, when my four sisters and I were at home with our mother and father and we were a family. I am not speaking of a particular time or memory, nor would I say I had a happy childhood, although sometimes I was happy, nor were we a happy family, although sometimes we were. But I was there again, fully immersed in the moment. In this visionary instant, my body, my mind, my senses were inseparable, a perfect fit with each other, and drifting upward out of my past, I felt such pure pleasure, such comfort, of a type I can't remember ever experiencing before at being back in that world of childhood. How rich our lives once were, how perfect when we were children. We didn't question our rightness on earth and knew nothing but what our senses brought us, even as we experienced the pain and incomprehension of being children. I found myself filled with wonder and gratefulness for the life I had had. I saw that my losses are commonplace among women my age, rather than extraordinary. I vowed then that I would say yes to everything. I told myself that if I wanted a new life, I would have to be at least open to the opportunities arriving on my doorstep.

Memory, to which I had chiefly paid no attention up to the tim of my mother's death in 1987, now became a puzzling but essen part of my life. On the one hand, I felt I should try to forget Peter my life with him on the ranch and the hay farm, because if I di

I was afraid I would slowly disintegrate into a shell of a living, breathing human being, someone merely waiting for death. On the other hand, the more I mulled over my past and the way I personally had lived it, the more it seemed to me essential that I not forget one detail of it, nor of the research I'd done, the years of reading, the endless, repetitive social events I'd attended, the small dramas and scandals I'd seen or heard about, or my own travails there with Peter. Over and over again, I thought of him rooting around in that small, overgrown cemetery surrounded by richly leafed trees I often couldn't name, in the low green mountains of Slovakia, on his knees, oblivious to me and to the young people with us, looking for something in the tall grass and the rotting and falling-over crosses, something he could not name, nor could I. I too wanted, and want very much, to pay homage to the past I lived and the people in it, and to the past before that, in Ireland and Scotland, and in France in the early seventeenth century. I was not alone in the world because so many family members were dead, and my husband too; I felt them with me often, and dreamt of them, and understood, slowly, dimly, that not only was I not alone in the world because they were dead, but that I was a part of a tapestry, both recent and ancient. Sean and his family had full, rich lives, a fact for which I could never be grateful enough, but in which I could never fully participate without intruding. I knew that I had to live my own life, whether I wanted to or not.

I had been a writer; for thirty years I had spent a large part of each day in my study working on a story, an article, a play, an essay, a book. If at first, after Peter died, I could barely hold a pencil and could not do the actual physical act of writing a word, I had eventually moved into something that resembled writing.

My conscience bothered me consistently when I was not working. After all those hard years of struggle and study, for many of them rising at 5 a.m. when Peter did and going straight to my desk, producing all those published books and articles, receiving the occasional grant to spur me in my work and once in a while an award,

I had fallen into laziness. I was failing my vocation, which had often felt sacred to me.

At the same time, I often lay awake and worried that my writing life was over, that perhaps I would never write a book or an essay or an article again. But if I couldn't write, I convinced myself that it wasn't my fault, was not some failure in me.

Still, the spiritual transformation I think now I was looking for did not come: the wholly new life; the new person. How many years had I dreamt of having all these city amenities immediately available to me without needing a hotel reservation, a plan, a five-hour drive each way to attend them? Why was I flagging only a few years into this new life? What was it I was missing?

I wanted to find a way to live that made me feel I was myself again, to live a life that was my own. I wanted an authentic life, that didn't feel as though I was wearing somebody else's ill-fitting clothing. I wanted to find my way back, after two confusing and difficult years, back to the self I had been, not when I left the university for the ranch when I was thirty-six, as I had been doing, but instead, the person I was at sixty-six when Peter died. I saw now that this was a mistake. I couldn't relive the past; I could only go on to a new future. I was no longer an eager thirty-six-year-old with an unimaginably long time before me. I was having to come to terms, finally, with the steady state of, in the midst of life, being old. From now on, my job would be discovering not just how to live the rest of my life, but how to live it while growing old.

In those early years in the city, thinking of the concept of home I sometimes remembered my mother talking to us when we we children about the big house on the farm in Manitoba that ' been her grandparents' on her father's side, of certain objec it, such as a very large china soup tureen and ladle, or the china pitchers and matching china basins in each bedroom. Her face softened when she remembered these items, gone many years before, forever, from her life, relics of a happy childhood, a life that before too many years turned into exile and too often led her into want. But she didn't dwell on this, and I chose not to dwell on my lost house either. When I was a child, we had moved a lot, yet I don't recall ever having the sense of having lost a home, because wherever we went I had my parents and my sisters still. "Home" went with us everywhere as long as we were all together. Since I grew up and went out into the world on my own, I have had many homes, many physical settings in which I built a life for myself. I suspect that for many women this is the case. It is what you bring to each place, what you invest each place with that sustains you.

Though the mouse-free place in which I now live turned out not to be paradise, I have my past to bolster me, those long years on the prairie with Peter that I cannot ever abandon. Even now, some mornings I wake up and gaze around my bedroom, and realize that for seven and more years I have been waiting for all this nonsense to stop so that I can go back to Peter, that this Calgary life has been only a momentary aberration. My real home is still waiting for me back in that house enclosed in the curve of the Frenchman River with the high hills behind it. I enjoy that momentary dream. I suppose that in time this bit of madness will fade, but part of me hopes that it will take a very long time to do so, the rest of my life. For it gives me great happiness and a sense of wholeness to know that I came from somewhere substantial and, in its way, beautiful.

I still have a strong sense of Peter waiting for me. It is surprising how often he works beside me at household tasks, or sleeps beside me in our bed. And yet, despite these fleeting dreams, I don't beve that we will be together in that Great Beyond; I don't for a ment believe that in the next life we just carry on with our old Still, he is a constant companion in my mind.

And yet, I wait for an ending; I wait for a degree of comprehension about those years that will enable me to place them in the story of my life — some story that I haven't yet written, because I can't yet draw conclusions; I can't fit things together nicely, in a clear order. A part of me wants very much to be able to do that; it seems to be part of the task I have set for myself for the remaining years of my life. Because rational thinking has never been my mode of coming to the most telling insights about my life, I haven't thought that one day this would happen to me. I have waited instead for a visionary moment when I would at last *see* and everything about my life would fall into place; I have waited, hopefully, for an explanatory dream.

Finally, as I neared the end of the writing of this book, I dreamt that the house on the prairie that Peter and I built and lived in together for thirty years was being flooded. The water was coming up from below at the centre of the house and flooding outward over the floor. It was also flowing, not copiously but inexorably from above, down the raw wood of the centre post that we — another woman and I — had managed to expose in our effort to find the place where the water was coming from. (Of course, there is no centre post in the real house.) The flow both from below and above was unrelenting, and the water itself was not frothy or bubbling or noisy, but silent and perfectly clear, yet it was strange in that it seemed to have a strength in it that tap water, river or lake water, or possibly even rain doesn't have.

The other woman was someone I seemed to be living with b[...] who had taken on the persona of one of my new urban-rural frie[...] from just before and after Peter's death. She didn't look muc[...] the real woman, was dressed in light grey slacks and a short-[...]

white blouse, and wore her perfectly smooth pale blonde hair in
a sophisticated French twist, a style the real woman would never
have worn. I never saw her face, just that perfect, gleaming hair,
but she was directing and helping me with the flood of water that
was spreading and spreading from the hidden source that we were
trying to find. I felt no grief, fear, or panic in the dream, just mild
concern because the rug was getting soaked, although we couldn't
see the water on the floor until we stepped in it and it soaked our
shoes and rose ankle-high. Awake, I struggled to remember where
I had seen that rug that I felt was one I knew intimately. Then I remembered that it was the one Peter and I put down in our bedroom
in the ranch house, as one of the very first tasks we did together in
the first months of our marriage.

As it happens, the dream insisted that the other woman was
Scandinavian, and I knew that would make the centre pole Yggdrasill (pronounced "ig'-druh-sill"), the holy tree, the world tree
of Norse legend. On waking, I had some vague memory of having
heard of this legend, but I knew none of the details. Years before
I had bought a copy of *The Penguin Book of Norse Myths: Gods of
the Vikings*, and now I searched my bookshelves until I located it
stuffed between Joseph Campbell's *Myths to Live By* and Carl Jung's
Man and His Symbols, none of which I'd looked at in years.

Yggdrasill, the book on Norse myths said, is the tree that "shel-
ters all creation," whose branches reach into the heavens and beyond. It has three great roots extending deep down into the earth,
ending no one knows where. Under the first root is a spring called
Hvergelmir, where a dragon gnaws corpses and does evil against
the tree; under the second root "flow[s] the well of Urd, the spring
of destiny," and nearby live the three maiden goddesses, or Norns:
rd, Verdandi, and Skuld (Fate, Being, and Necessity). The third
t goes into the realm of the frost giants and under it is a spring
led by "wise Mimir," "and the water in that well gave insight to
who tasted it. . . . Odin had given one eye for a single draught

from it. He won immense knowledge there and with it the thirst for yet greater wisdom."

The dream seemed to be that last, fitting comment that I was waiting for, telling me as it did that I had had the fullest possible life all those years that I lived in the wilds of the country among the cattle and horses, the birds and animals, the wind, the grass, and the stars.

And yet, I don't think that my path, strange as it might have been (although I think it is closer to commonplace), is necessarily the right one for every woman left in late mid-life to make her own way in the world, alone, lonely, and dealing with the deepest grief. I don't want to set myself up as an example to be followed; life is not like that. But sometimes on the streets I see women, strangers I guess to be about my age, walking by and I see something missing from their faces and their eyes that is more than the effect of growing old. Granted, immense sadness, loneliness, and also age fade our faces and melt and dissolve our once svelte lines. But this absence I've seen seems to me to be caused by the flickering light of a spirit going out.

I believe that once you find yourself — your real self — still there inside that old-woman exterior, and you begin to see yourself as *alive* and, indeed, as *worthy* of a life, a real life (instead of living in a steady state only as a person nearing death), that drabness will slowly disappear as the spirit flares up again. Grief has its own time-table; grief requires from the sufferer, besides its measure of misery that must be endured, careful, wide-ranging, and intense thought both about the sufferer's life, and life itself. Grief's claws grasp deep and cling; it is only the face that, eventually, turns toward things-as-they-are-now, and the future, that can cause those claws to release

But no one knows better than I how hard it is to do that, a how much courage, indeed, as James Hillman has written in *Force of Character and the Lasting Life*, how much pure fo character it takes.

8

The Gift

It had been determined by fate that I would not live in a house again, but only in rented apartments or condos because I could not handle cutting the grass; managing the trees, flower beds, and decorative shrubs; or, in winter, shoveling the snow or breaking the sidewalk ice, or fixing eaves troughs or roof shingles, and I already knew from life on the land that getting somebody to do the work would be harder than doing it myself. I would never again even be able to open a normal, ordinary door onto a backyard with a lawn and a lawn chair; I would not again grow a vegetable garden, or plant a flower be nor would I ever again be able to wander the prairie at will, g any direction that appealed to me, or find Aboriginal artifac features, or routinely see wild animals from my kitchen wi From now on my connection to nature would be only in m on asphalt paths through manicured parks with hundreds of others strolling the same paths at the same time. Or so I thought.

Once arrived in the city, I had also thought that I would spend my usual walking-in-nature time in the vast Nose Hill Park, a wild prairie park of historical significance, with features going back to pre-contact times — it is the very large grassy hill visitors can see from the windows of their plane as they land or take off — the obvious place for me to recover some of what I'd lost in terms of being in the wild. But, as it turned out, Nose Hill Park was miles from where I lived, and could only be reached on the city's system of freeways and major feeder roads, roads I simply was not ready to drive at the time. I looked longingly at it whenever I was at the airport but have walked it only twice in eight years, with people who wanted to walk it with me. Instead, I got out the city map and found the large parks near where I lived.

I was surprised to see how wild they were. One of them, Fish Creek Park, has Fish Creek, a mountain stream, flowing through it, which is in some seasons dangerously wide and fast. During the great flood of 2013 it gouged out sections of the paved walking paths and knocked out not only trees but the smaller footbridges, not to mention picnic sites and playgrounds. In other seasons it is reduced to placid pools connected only by a thread of water. One day, as I was walking down a path, an ambulance or police siren went off somewhere in the near distance, and suddenly the woods around me set up an answering howl, and I realized to my amazement that they were full of coyotes.

The other park I began to walk in runs around the city's reservoir, created in 1932 by the damming of the Elbow River to provide water supply for the city. Part of the park is called the Weaselhead tural Area (after a Native leader), and includes a long, more or circular looping trail that, near where I live, runs from just d Rockyview Hospital, then through a residential neighbour- nd next, an outdoor shopping centre. Along this section the path is nearly always busy with people, and it is tame — except for the time I came up the path at the back of the shopping centre and in the midst of dozens of placid strollers a buck deer with a magnificent rack stood there, head up, looking both startled and bewildered as we all gave him a wide berth. Farther west, though, except on the very best summer days, the number of walkers thins and the path goes for a few kilometres through forest and into an area where there is a long, high bridge that crosses the Elbow River and a beautiful, wet, and green wild area.

One day my son, running there at the extreme western boundary of the park, saw a mother bear with two cubs break out of the woods on one side of the path and cross just ahead of him to disappear into the woods on the other side. Another day, as I walked down near the water's edge, I came within an inch of putting my foot down in a pile of berry-pit-laden fresh bear scat. Every once in a while a bear will invade the neighbourhoods adjacent to the park, and parks and animal protection people along with the police and/or fire department will have to come out and spend a couple of hours trying to corral the bear, usually getting it first down from a tree, before tranquillizing it and taking it into the backcountry.

I suppose a committed ecologist would have to say that the Weaselhead is a degraded wilderness, because in the part in which most people walk, there have been a few incursions by "tame" plants: caraganas have moved in, as well as some versions of flowering plants that must have come from the nearby neighbourhoods, and studying assiduously one small area off the path, I realized that it had once been a homesteading site. Still, do the animals care if the tree that gives them shelter was imported from the Russian steppes or was native to the area? And the weary sunstruck walk is happy to rest in the shade of a non-native tree.

To be fair, I once came upon members of the parks' staff small field digging out a stand of plants they knew would do age to the area's native biodiversity. I am all for trying to a pristine wilderness — don't mistake me about that — but a less-than-perfect wilderness can be most valuable too. I see it as an improvement over a park with mown grass, carefully sown flower beds, and a clump of trees planted for an aesthetically pleasing effect. Not that there isn't a place for that kind of park, or even that I don't enjoy one — I love them too — but I tell myself, this is Calgary in the New World, it is not Versailles.

Calgarians often say — it is an article of faith here — that the best thing about living in the city is how close you are to nature, usually meaning the mountain parks, of which the first is Banff, only an hour or so away. They pay less attention to the parks I'm writing about, that have brought me such pleasure. Yet I am sure I'm not the only park walker who sometimes gazes with longing eyes across the chain-link fence mostly hidden by foliage and tall grass to the meadows and rising treed blue-green hills on the other side where First Nations people, the Tsuu T'ina, have their reserve, a place that looks as if little of it has been despoiled. Nonetheless, heading west on the Weaselhead each day, I am walking toward the mountains that rise along the skyline, snow-peaked, or purple and blue, rugged, wild, and stirring up that endless yearning of the human for the true wildness and purity that we all crave.

One day, in my loneliness, I paused in my walk to lean against a conifer tree that had grown about a foot from the path and that had no bushes surrounding it, so that I had only to step to the right and ut my head and shoulder against it, while I sighed like a lovesick racter in an Elizabethan drama, lost utterly, for that moment, in adness. The tree trunk was only about a foot in diameter and for er not tall, not more than maybe twelve feet high, so a young stood there, the tree and I, in perfect silence. I cannot recall my thoughts, but I straightened and stepped away, about a foot from the trunk, but so that I was still under the branches. Suddenly, a pine cone fell and hit me smack on the top of my head. I am sure I laughed, feeling that the tree was acknowledging my presence. Then another cone fell, and another, then two or three more at the same time, and then, as I stood there in surprise and pleasure, the tree shed around me its entire load of cones. It was like standing under a waterfall as the cones fell all around me, dropping without much speed, ceaselessly, gently, none of them now touching me in their downward passage. I stood motionless until the last cone had hit the asphalt path; I could hardly move for wonder.

As I know that most of the world doesn't believe that such things happen — that is, a tree communing with a human — I decided to ask if it was standard practice for such a tree to drop all its cones at once. Nobody I asked knew; the "experts" seemed surprised by the question, as if it hadn't occurred to them to wonder how long it took a single tree to shed its cones. Weeks? Months? Days? Hours? But all at once? I gave up asking. It was then that I began to believe that nature is as much itself in the city as it is in the place I'd come from, miles from the nearest residence.

On another occasion, in a different park, when again I was alone and the path was otherwise empty of people, three snakes crossed in front of me. They were just garter snakes of differing sizes, but I had never seen so much as a hint of a snake in that park before, although, of course, I knew that they had to be there somewhere. And so when the first one came gliding out of the undergrowth I took note, a sort of hmm! And then the second one, and then the third a few feet farther on, and I thought, either it the time of day (about five p.m.) and they are going for water, am seeing things. I try not to let the mind-set of the scientif oriented taint my own worldview, as if there has to be an e tion for everything. Is there a mind in nature, a consciousn a purposefulness? Is there no such thing as a soul?

The contemporary German philosopher Georg Misch wrote that when people "find themselves not congruent with the cultures they live in, they seek to regain the harmony and inner tranquility of a right relationship with nature and the spiritual world." The older I get, the more I think about my own life, the more I think Misch's statement is a final truth. It was certainly true of my life on the grasslands when I was Peter's wife and found that I could not easily make my way into the lives of the local women, and I began to wonder if I was to blame for this.

I understand now that my need for solitude to write was part of what caused this to happen. I am often surprised by people who think they live solitary lives, but who seem to me to not know what real solitude is. Solitude is when year after year nobody, or almost nobody, drops in just to see you. Settler women without children knew this kind of solitude, isolated as they were on homesteads far from neighbours or villages. I've come to accept my need for solitude in itself as part of my nature. More and more I notice how urban writers and artists seem to be intent on experiencing that kind of true solitude by making arrangements to go into a cabin in the woods and stay there all alone for a week or a month, or who seek solitude through religious retreats and living in religious communities. These people go into nature by choice, knowing instinctively that it is in nature that the human can best find herself. I think that the two are interwoven in the search for a quiet soul and for spiritual answers: solitude and nature. During my walks on the prairie, I struggled hard to find my authentic self, the real self, the one that I had had, perhaps, from before my birth. One of the effects of this determination to find some kind of rock-bottom certainty, which apparently couldn't be found in the cultural institutions of the "real" world, was to give myself permission in that walking in nature, to let my intuition take the lead.

What is intuition? It seems mostly to suddenly strike us without on our part. Intuition is light, nearly weightless, at least it is for me. It involves listening to your inner world, after you have subdued the steady, omnipresent mutter of consciousness, so that the urges of intuition have room to come forward and be noticed. It takes courage, too, to follow those urges, to slow your thinking down. There is little room for science in intuition: Intuition admits of no explanation. But it also allows your self-awareness to come forward. And it can mollify grief.

What I listen for is not the music of birds, not the susurration of leaves, or the wind in the branches; I am listening for spirit. Mostly I don't hear it. What it is is a returning attention to me, not a sound, never anything I can see, not a voice. It is, simply, *Attention*. With it is a waiting, as if whatever is attending to me and my desire to connect with it is waiting for me to speak in some meaningful way, although I never have anything to say. I suppose I could ask, *Who are you?* But I wouldn't expect an answer, and I'm sure I wouldn't get one anyway. Yesterday, walking, I thought that it is almost enough just to know it is sometimes there; that its mere presence is reassuring.

But an understanding that I had been mulling over for years came flooding through me, as if that very spirit had been waiting for the right moment to let me know: I understood, finally, that indeed a life in nature is the better one, the more natural one, the one that allows us more easily to be fully human, and to find our humanity. It was a clear and irrevocable understanding. Yet in the next instant, I saw again the theatres, the concert halls, the cathedrals, the universities, the vast possibilities for the companionship of, conversations with, like-minded people. This time, the urban values fell into their rightful place. They became secondary to the force of a life lived mindfully in nature. And yet, I and most of the world remain in cities; for most of us there isn't a choice. And a life lived in nature is always, at some time, a lonely one. Humans also need companionship of their own kind, just as they need cultural activities to help the soul grow.

One sunny quiet September day in Calgary as I walked on a path just above the water's edge, I came to a place where a thin screen of trees between me and the reservoir had opened so that I was looking out at the sun-dazzled water as if through a picture frame made of yellow and green cottonwood leaves. I was filled with sheer pleasure at the beauty I was looking at. I walked on two or three steps, and in one of those moments of lightness when intuition takes over and the brain loses control, without even hesitating I stopped and backed up those same two or three steps, not taking my eyes off the water, and then, in the middle of the leafy frame, a fish jumped. A large fish, spraying an arc of brilliant water and vanishing soundlessly in less than a second.

Never in five years of almost daily gazing out at the reservoir had I ever seen a fish jump. I didn't really believe there were fish in it, even though I often passed fishermen. I kept on walking, thinking that as soon as I saw a fisherman I would ask him what kind of a fish that was. But all the fishermen were busy, or were behind a thicker stand of trees, or too far down at the water's edge. Finally, on a bend where I had never before seen anyone fishing, a tall, slender, youngish man stood reeling in his line. I stopped, excused myself for disturbing him, and asked him what kind of a fish would jump.

"You saw a fish jump?" he asked, in evident surprise. As if getting a grip on his thoughts, he named all the kinds of fish in the reservoir, then, shifting again as if just remembering the question, said it would have been a trout. "They jump for flies," he told me. I thanked him. Searching for a polite remark on which to leave, I said, "I just like . . . to know things." In a clear, strong voice, he answered, "I like to know things too." By this time he had packed his fishing equipment and was beginning to climb up the rocks toward me, and I saw that he was a First Nations man, the first I had seen fishing there.

I walked away, for a moment feeling that the universe and I were in near-perfect communication. I cherish that simple memory and am comforted by it. Calm can return if you are alone in nature, nature having its way of bringing to mind thoughts of eternal matters.

That *listening*, that *attention*, certainly doesn't happen every time I go out, nor do I ever go out for a walk with that one experience on my mind as a destination. I go out for other reasons: to enjoy nature as nature, whether or not that includes nature as spirit, because, after all, trees, grass, shrubs, flowers — all are alive, and I never forget that Aboriginal people believe all things in nature to be enspirited, and I think that myself.

Some years ago, in perhaps the last year of Peter's life, early one cold winter morning as we drove away from the hay farm on the mundane chore of going to the dentist in Medicine Hat, we were heading north on a road that was little more than a trail, snow banked up on each side of the truck, and fields of unspoiled snow stretching out to the edge of the glistening hills, one of us looked back — I don't know why or who — and gasped, causing the other to look back. I know Peter slowed the truck, I think he stopped it for a few seconds. A cloud of white ice fog or icy mist, opaque but radiant, was moving as we watched, from the east toward our house to rest over it, completely encompassing it so that all we could see was the cloud. It was shot with tiny rainbows like half-hidden jewels; it glowed a numinous white. It didn't strike the road in fro the hills behind, or the neighbour's house a half mile to the ea the dilapidated barn to the west, just our house and yard. I alive and glowing with light. Now we both gasped; neithe though used to sun dogs and even in extreme cold to mo had ever seen such a thing. That it had covered and surrounded our house surprised and just possibly frightened me a little, if not Peter. I was so full of awe that the word *celestial* came into my mind. Being practical people (or at least Peter was), though, we drove on, watching through the rear-view mirrors until we no longer could see it.

I so wanted it to be a blessing for his dream — now achieved — of saving his grass. Although there had been considerable dissent in our area about this, as I mentioned earlier, and we had to pass many tests, a project of this size and particular nature not having been done in our province before, most of Canada had been thrilled, and the First Nations people of the area had been happy about it. Peter had become a hero. A few years later he died, but not before a gentleman who has been for many years important in conservation work came to say good-bye to him and told him, "You have changed the face of Canada."

On the day of Peter's funeral, once it was over and as many as fifty people had come out to the hay farm to hold an informal post-funeral wake, voices out in the yard began to call those of us in the house to "Look! Quick, come outside!" One of our number had, using his drum, already sung Peter an honour song, and afterward we had dispersed through the house and yard. Now we congregated again in the yard; it was nearing twilight, cloudless, and the vast sky was intensely luminous as it can be in Western Canada on a hot, late-summer evening. We faced the west, where the sun, hovering on the radiant horizon along the line of the hills, had turned blue. We were stunned by this event. We watched qui-etly without anyone speculating why it was happening, until it had sappeared below the western hills.

In the first year after I moved to the city to live, I dreamt Peter ome home. We were at the ranch and I opened the door of the ch house that he and his sisters had been raised in and there standing out on the prairie in his ragged old work clothes

and his battered and stained grey Stetson, grinning at me — I in
the house, he on the prairie that extended all around him, cream-
coloured grass melding into soft blues and aquas in the far distance.
I was pretty angry with him because, as I said to him, he had been
so rude as to miss his own funeral and I scolded him for it as he
grinned back at me like an incorrigible schoolboy. He said he'd been
on a fishing trip at Chitek Lake (a place in northern Saskatchewan
neither of us had ever been) with — he named two local men. Then
I suddenly remembered what had actually happened and I said in
horror, one hand flying up to hold my head, "Oh, my God! I sold
the hay farm!" Already I was going through possibilities about how
to get it back even as I was terrified that it would be impossible. But
Peter said instantly, himself again, no longer grinning, but fully casual, utterly dismissive, as if such a thing didn't matter at all, "Yeah,
yeah, I know. It's okay." And in the end it has been.

Epilogue

Starry Sky

I think it could be said of this book, as Joan Didion says of hers, "This book is about grief." And yet, how do you write about grief in the singular, in the present, as it happens? Grief is too big to write about that way, and so writers tend to write small anecdotes, to describe the past with the deceased in everyday ways, and by doing this hope to create the larger picture. So I have tried to do, yet I feel at the moment of writing this that I haven't fully succeeded, leaning, perhaps, too far toward the beautiful and the romantic, leaving out the grit and ugline and pain of death.

When someone you love dies, everything gets mixed up experience a conflict of emotions: grief, loss, self-pity, love passion. You must also deal with the reactions of others. T' bination for a widow is terrible. This before she has ever become a widow, when her husband is still alive and opening his eyes to gaze at her with an expression in them she cannot read, as if he is seeing her for the first time in his life; as if in his dying he has gained the ability to read a soul, and what he finds there amazes him. This is not love or pity or sympathy. This is a man, for the first time in his life, as it ends, coming at last *to see*, to see what he never before in his life had been able to see.

And still he does not speak. Does not at that moment of his dying feel a need to speak, or a duty to speak, while the widow holds a cloth to his forehead, whispers in his ear, holds his hand, strokes his cheek. He is beyond that kind of connection; he is looking, is already partly there, into a future no one else can see. You, moments from your widowhood, can see he is gone from you already even though he is still breathing and his hand and forehead and cheek are warm. You can see that whatever the others around his bed were to him, whatever you were to him, is over. The world becomes hollow; you are hollowed; in that density of black, that cavern full of darkness, there is not even an echo. Something is over. Something has ended, and there is nothing — *nothing at all* — to fill that black cavern that is your interior. It will be such a long time, years even, before anything slips in, and then something else, and then something else, until the cavern that is your interior narrows, shrinks at the edges, may even close. But the closing is fragile. It tears easily, it disintegrates minutely if examined; it is better not to examine it. It is probably better not to write books about it. But what is a writerly person to do, after all? When she has made such examination, such conjecture, such thought, how she lives her life, how *she* gets through *her* allotted span.

Time passes. Years pass. She moves — no, I move to a city another province. I start again. Lesson number one in grief: never start again, although you think you do. I tell everyone have started again and I know that from the outside it I have started again. I live on the third floor now, and although I have a balcony that overlooks a green space where all spring, summer, and fall soccer players of all ages and genders shout and stumble and run like fury, and whistles blow and blow again, if I want to touch the ground I have to put on appropriate clothing, grab my keys, walk down the hall, and either take three sets of stairs or the elevator, and walk through a heavy door if I want to feel the branch of a tree, or sniff a flower up close. Age teaches resignation; grief teaches itself to *be*, to just *be*, because it turns out that it can't be outrun or forgotten.

I can never forget, for example, in our last days in a hospital in Saskatoon, a busy, noisy, much too big hospital where I was to be Peter's advocate and his protector, and where, like all patients, I — we — had become the victims of the system, of protocol, of the machinery of such a place, and I had — although I was there nearly all the time for a dozen or more hours each day — once again missed the visit of the surgeon who was to perform (or would not, as would be the case) Peter's surgery, and the nurses couldn't, were not allowed to tell me anything at all, and I had been brave for days and months and kept tears to myself, and worked to be clipped and sane, clear-eyed and intelligent, Peter told me something the surgeon had said that he did not under-stand and, baffled and angry, I said, "I will find out what is going on." And I marched out of his room and down to the nursing station, opened my mouth to speak in that firm, clever persona I had adopted as the one that would work best in this environment, and instead began to cry. I became a fountain of tears. I sobbed so hard I couldn't breathe. I was humiliated by my own weakness, by my clear plea for pity for *me*, not for Peter, but I could not stop. The nurse to whom I had been trying to speak came around th desk and put her arms around me, other staff came and held too, and talked over my head about what to do, about how to the doctor. I was ashamed of myself — it was the very thin mother most hated, wallowing in self-pity, losing your dig public. True, I have not forgotten this moment, but when I do recall it, I try to forgive myself. You have to give in to grief to move through it and beyond.

Eventually, I'm finding, old griefs become mingled with the loss of Peter: the loss of my first husband through divorce, and the divided life we created for our child, the fact that I'll never again see my father or my mother or two of my dear sisters, and other smaller sorrows. They bundle together and become the sorrow of life, of living. They become the human condition, at last. They become even, in a painful way, deeply beautiful, like an embroidered wall-hanging from the twelfth century, the colours faded, the edges a little hazy now, the glint of gold threads no longer blazing, but soft and delicately gleaming. My past, my personal deaths, remind me of the most beautiful cathedral I was ever in, not St. Paul's in Rome or even Notre Dame in Paris, but the stone church in Kirkwall, on Orkney's main island, St. Magnus's, begun in 1137 and finished three hundred years later. As I walked down its main aisle, pausing to gaze around me, it seemed to me that the surface of the sandstone of which it was built was turning soft and hazy, the beams of light from the side windows the light of centuries earlier, filled with dully glinting dust motes, the whole interior as if I had walked into an ancient dream of beauty itself.

We experience death on so many levels. The hard reality of the physical act of dying, our own need for self-pity and silent grieving, society's need for commemoration — each person must make her own understanding, her own tapestry of experience. Nine years have passed since that day in the palliative ward when I said good-bye to Peter, and if I have learned anything about grief *t is that the people you have loved in life are still there in death; at is, through dreams and memories, and sudden flashes of understanding, you know they are still there with you. I often think even if you forget them — although who could do that? — o not forget you. Loss, then, even grievous loss, as time slowly passes transforms itself into a continuing relationship that provides a gentle, wondering comfort.

In the last months of 2015, I received an email from the agency that now owns and manages what was the Butala cattle ranch that I first saw in 1975, the Nature Conservancy of Canada. One of its officials was writing to tell me that a difficult decision had to be made: whether to tear down the family home on the site, allow it to deteriorate slowly into dust, or possibly find somebody who might be willing to try to raise enough money to rebuild it. In subsequent communications the last option was dropped. With that first careful email came a photograph of the house yard taken by a professional photographer, at night, with special equipment (time lapse, etc.), with what I think was the aurora lighting the low northern sky, and above that, a plethora of stars, millions and millions of them, going far, far back into the unknowable, unreachable, not even quite imaginable cosmos and that, far, far out at its distant edges, can only end in myth and dream. For all the work that had been done in the way of professional photographers recording the place for one reason or another, nobody had ever produced a picture of the barn and house and yard that so brought out its genuine beauty, the way that it was situated, a tiny human habitation, hardly a pinprick on that vast tract of grass-covered hills and under the unlimited, bounteous, star-studded sky.

All day I was sad and couldn't put my finger on why, but as it was November 11, Remembrance Day, I thought that must be the reason. But then the truth caught up with me: it was the thought of that house being destroyed, disappearing from the face of the earth.

All day I kept seeing the green of the grass in the yard in the photo, the red of the barn, the L shape of the old, unlovely house.

and that enormous, star-filled sky. All day I lived inside the other memories the picture brought me: how far you would have to go on horseback or on foot to get to another occupied house, how empty the hills were, with the wind always sweeping through or dancing around you, as you rode slowly across the grass, through wide draws, and that great sky there above you, the horizon so low that the sky was all around you. I remembered the lichen-covered rocks nestling in the dry yellow grass, bright red, orange, gold, pale green, or white or black, slashes and patches, unexpected, peering up through the grass, and the purity of the colours filling you with delight: the tiny exquisitely designed flowers mostly white or yellow — yarrow and buffalo beans or locoweed or prickly pears — but with the occasional blue of the flax flower or even sometimes the mauve-blue of the penstemon; the tiny scarlet mallow; the creamy wild onion, never to be confused with the lookalike death camas that kills cattle; or the brilliant flare of goldenrod; the rose-fading-to-pink of the gumbo primrose. I remembered the scent of the wild carried on the wind, of the grasses and forbs — the wild roses, the primroses, the various aromatic, peppery sages, and the sweet dusty wild grasses — especially in the spring.

The more years I was there, the more personal it was, the more intimate. The spirits that lived there — were they the ones the Romans of the ancient world called *genii loci*? — seemed always with me.

I suppose, gazing at that picture, that I ached too for Peter, for the time we spent there together, how close we were in the early days. How I loved him for his easy courage that was mostly plain old knowledge shaped by common sense, his competency that seemed to me at times to reach a kind of brilliance, as if in a crisis his brain would crack open in a new place (that's how the light gets *out*). I was awed by this capacity in him; it made me love him more. This, and the way he left me to think my own thoughts, so that at last, beside him, I learned how to be myself.

I am still endlessly grateful. That I was *there*, all those many,

many years, out there on the land and under that boundless sky, living among animals and birds and growing things, and in the constantly changing weather, this with someone who could show me and teach me about such a life and how to live it. Someone who was so familiar with it that he was himself part of it. There could be no greater gift to a single individual.

Now, battle-scarred and weary, to quote storytellers everywhere and through time, I am grateful for those years. Without them I would be some other person. In those sometimes even *terrible* years I was learning how deep the shadow goes: how implacable, how relentless and ancient the larger shadow in the world, how equally wide and deep the human soul. Whatever the cost, this is worth knowing: how, in the middle of life, nature is consolation, solace, friend, spiritual guide, and teacher.

Bison herd on the Old Man On His Back Prairie
and Heritage Conservation Area.

Acknowledgements

One of my happiest moments with regard to my rural past came when I was reading in Swift Current and eight or nine people, all retirees, who had been my neighbours when I first went into the Divide-Claydon area to live in the mid-seventies, came to hear me. I found them still a warm-hearted, lively bunch, and I was very touched to see them. I thank them also for reasons that go back to when I first met them and heard from my husband the stories of their families and their land, and learned from the women their forbearance and quiet resolution.

Juxtaposed with them are the urban people who in the late nineties began to move into Eastend. From them I saw in certain ways a re-enactment of my own efforts to come to terms with a local society that rarely bent to meet a newcomer halfway. They provided me with friendship and the return of an ease that I hadn't felt in years. I thank all of them — those who stayed, and those who left — for this, and for bringing into such sharp focus the differences between rural/small-town and urban ways of seeing the world.

I thank also the Nature Conservancy of Canada people, who saw the possibility in Peter's vision, and who fell as in love with the land as Peter and I were. Of these, John Grant was the first.

Others were Wayne Harris, who sadly died shortly thereafter in a farm accident; the inimitable Lorne Scott; Conrad Olson; and Sue Michalsky, the first project manager. The first of the NCC board to visit was Elva Kyle, and many donors, beyond the peerless Weston family, came, and Jack Messer, then of SaskPower, a pivotal player in the fundraising and planning. I know that I will wake in the night as those names I've forgotten from twenty years ago return to haunt me and I ask forgiveness. Without them there would be no Old Man On His Back Prairie and Heritage Conservation Area.

In writing this memoir I have drawn on some of my other non-fiction books for information and inspiration: *Coyote's Morning Cry*, *Lilac Moon*, *The Perfection of the Morning*, and *Wild Stone Heart*, in which the quotation from Greg Grace originally appeared, on page 129. I also quote a remark by J. M. Coetzee found in David Atwell's *J. M. Coetzee and the Life of Writing: Face to Face with Time* (New York: Viking, 2015), on page 209.

Through all of these books, including this memoir, I have had the good fortune to work with editor Phyllis Bruce CM, to whom I owe tremendous gratitude for her brilliant editor's eye, her expertise, and her unfailing wisdom. My agent, Jackie Kaiser, has been unflagging and invaluable in her perspicacity and her support. I thank them both.

My son, Sean Hoy, daughter-in-law, Carol, and my two grandchildren, Declan and Maeve, keep me on track. Sean, an actor and writer himself, has always supported me in my work, as I have tried to support him in his. My sisters, Cynthia and Deanna, themselves writers, have provided me with invaluable advice and encouragement, as did our youngest sister, Kathleen, to whom this book is dedicated. I cherish my close bond with our sister Sheila, who died in 1998. I thank all of them for their steadfastness and caring. Our mother, Margaret Amy (Graham)

Le Blanc, still speaks in our ears every single day, and I thank her and acknowledge all the ways in which she shaped us. I thank, too, Peter's mother, Alice Butala, especially for her example of bravery and innovativeness.

About Peter's great gift to me, I let this book speak.

Bibliography

Athill, Diana. *Somewhere Towards the End.* London: Granta, 2008.

Auster, Paul, and Coetzee, J. M. *Here and Now: Letters 2008–2011.* New York: Viking, 2013.

Butala, Sharon. *Coyote's Morning Cry: Meditations & Dreams from a Life in Nature.* Toronto: HarperCollins Canada, 1995.

———. *Lilac Moon: Dreaming of the Real West.* Toronto: Harper-Collins Canada, 2005.

———. *The Perfection of the Morning: An Apprenticeship in Nature.* Toronto: HarperCollins Canada, 1994.

———. *Wild Rose.* Regina, Saskatchewan: Coteau Books, 2015.

———. *Wild Stone Heart: An Apprentice in the Fields.* Toronto: HarperCollins Canada, 2000.

Crossley-Holland, Kevin. *The Penguin Book of Norse Myths: Gods of the Vikings.* London: Penguin Books, 1980.

Didion, Joan. *The Year of Magical Thinking*. New York: Alfred A. Knopf, 2005.

Drabble, Margaret. *The Witch of Exmoor*. Toronto: McClelland & Stewart, 1996.

Heilbrun, Carolyn. *The Last Gift of Time: Life Beyond Sixty*. New York: The Dial Press, 1997.

Hillman, James. *The Force of Character and the Lasting Life*. New York: Random House, 1999.

Ingram, Jay. *The End of Memory: A Natural History of Aging and Alzheimer's*. Toronto: HarperCollins Canada, 2015.

Kaye, Frances W. *Goodland: A Meditation and History on the Great Plains*. Edmonton, Alberta: Athabasca University Press, 2011.

Laurence, Margaret. *The Stone Angel*. Toronto: McClelland & Stewart, 1964.

McWilliams, Candia. *What to Look for in Winter: A Memoir in Blindness*. New York: HarperCollins Publishers, 2012. (First published in England by Jonathan Cape, 2010.)

Naipaul, V. S. *The Enigma of Arrival: A Novel in Five Sections*. New York: Alfred A. Knopf, 1987.

Small, Helen. *The Long Life*. Toronto: Oxford University Press, 2007.